# Blue Popsicles

## NeAnni Y. Ife

**xulon** PRESS

# With Gratitude

෴

To all of the Orphans who passed through the Gates. It was, and will always be our Home.

To Al and Nancy Lane for your friendship, encouragement, and support; and for seeing what should have been obvious, yet was overlooked. Hotep!

To Anna Marie McCormick Stark for more than 40 years of love and laughter, and for being, as you put it, my Spirit Sister. Pray for Peace!

To Jerrie L. Bascome McGill, for being my mother/sister/friend, and for always knowing, saying, and doing the right things.

To my surviving siblings, Corine, Reco, Betty, Dean, Bill, Bob, Ed, and Daved, my thanks and my love, always.

And in the tradition of saving the best for last, to my children, Anthony W. Gibson and Tanya J. Gibson, I couldn't have done it without you. There would have been no reason to try. Love you, ever and ever.

# Preface

ॐ

Childhood, we are told, is a very special period in life: a time of innocence, unbridled curiosity, and wonderment. The things seen through a child's eyes or felt from a child's heart are perceived at face value, and may not be understood at all. The naiveté of a child is what allows words, thoughts, and actions to flow without much regard to the consequences that result. Childhood is suppose to be a time of unrestrained joy, happiness, exploration, and the ability to embrace fantasy and dreams.

As children, we should be encouraged to dream our dreams without regard to whether they are politically correct, socially acceptable, or could pass a grammar or spell check. We can dream in black and white or in all the colors of the rainbow. The pictures we draw and the world we see as children often defy convention. And it is this unfettered perception that gives the child's eye-view its raw beauty and priceless value.

But childhood, like all phases of life, is injected with concepts and actions that can interrupt and destroy our will to dream, to imagine our possibilities, and our pursuit of self-discovery. The curves we are thrown cannot be seen or foreseen and can induce hurt, anger, hate, self-doubt, self-pity, pain, and injustice. Perhaps these emotions are to give us a sense of perspective, to know the difference between the opposites: love vs. hate, good vs. evil, right vs. wrong, greed vs. generosity, etc. And when the negative opposites that we endure appear out of balance with the positives, we begin to ask ourselves why: Why me? Why this? Why now?

NeAnni Ife has been asking these questions since age six, and the answers have never been satisfactory because there is truly no answer or response to explain why humans perpetrate inhumanity against each other. She asked those who brought the pain she endured, she asked God, she asked herself-why? An adequate answer is elusive.

Her mother, Ellen Gibson, found a simple cure for pain: a blue Popsicle. That cool, icy treat that could some how soothe the hurt right out of a scraped knee, take the swelling out of a bump on the head, or miraculously close the wound from a nail in the foot. Of course, the manufacturers of Popsicles offer no claims to the healing powers of their product, but in the Gibson household it was a commonly accepted fact that blue Popsicles were a cure-all. Perhaps Ellen Gibson understood all too well the psychology of childhood imagination and the ability to believe in something.

At the age of six, NeAnni and most of her siblings were sent to the Ohio Soldiers' and Sailors' Orphans' Home in Xenia, Ohio, where she lived for eleven years. Though she experienced many instances of humiliation, degradation, and pain [negative opposites] at the hands of supervisors and other officials at the Home, she also experienced kindness, encouragement, and inspiration [positive opposites]. She finds a haven for her spirit in the African Methodist Episcopal Church where she is taken because, "We don't know what would happen if we took a colored child to a white church." The black church becomes the spiritual and psychological antidote she consumes to ward off her feelings of confusion and the irreconcilable differences she has with those whose manifest purpose seems to be to remind her that being black is no cause for celebration, or even acknowledgement. Ife's experiences in the church and its role as comforter, protector, and builder of self-affirmation symbolize the significance of the church in the black community: the blue Popsicle for our spiritual ailments.

Peer bonding became a necessary survival technique. The reassurance and support the Orphans gave each other allowed them to cope. It also let them know that they were not alone in the world. Relationships forged among the Orphans became strong and all important, transcending race and gender. We see what Ife is telling us about weathering the storms that engulf us, and how very important it is to have 'big arms' to wrap around us.

The OS&SO Home became the physical and psychological prison for Ife and many of her friends, whose only crime was "being born into families who, for whatever reasons, couldn't take care of us." Thus a Twist of fate becomes a criminal act, punishable by abuse at the hands of the guardians [or is it guards] who for the most part misplaced love, compassion, and fair discipline with indifference, cruelty, and disregard for respect and humanity that should have been accorded to the children they were charged to protect.

Ife understands the source of her frustration and pain, and seeks to withdraw into a shell, like the turtle she saw on a field trip to the institution's farm. The turtle's hard shell is its protector when it is frightened. Ife was seven years old when she discovered the turtle's defense mechanism. Her journey through childhood to adolescence and adulthood has given her the perspective to reach beyond retribution and fear and to seek reconciliation and forgiveness. She discovered a cure for the pain that interrupted her will to dream and to free the person inside of her. She ultimately makes a conscious decision to define her own being, to leave bitterness in someone else's cup, and rise above the resentment and contempt she harbored for those responsible for her pain.

The remedy was to go inside herself; not to hide like the

turtle, but to bring forth the person she knew was there; to allow the light to shine on her, so she could learn, create, write, raise children, give love, receive love, ask forgiveness, and forgive. These things she has done, and a lot more. Ms. Ife restored her will to dream, to fantasize about what could be, and to set out to make it happen. The eyes and heart of a child are always within us, which helps the positive opposites to prevail.

And if you ever fall down and scrape your knee, or run into a wall and bump your head, just reach for Ellen Gibson's cure-all: blue Popsicles.

—Allan C. Lane, January 2002

# Contents

ॐ

# Chapter 1

ॐ

Paisley was a quiet, tree-lined, two-block street in Dayton, Ohio, bounded by First and Dakota Streets. On the Dakota side was the levee that harnessed the Miami River, the line of demarcation that separated the coloreds from the whites. Most of the yards were dotted with flowers and shade tress. A few sprouted fruit trees and grapevines as well.

The houses on our street were mostly two-story frames, with a few brick houses sprinkled throughout. Ours was a red-shingle, two-bedroom, two-story with few amenities. One could stand at the front door and look straight through the front room, the middle room, the kitchen, and out the back door. Both bedrooms were upstairs.

On the landing at the bottom of the steps was a trap door that led to the cellar. I don't remember ever going down there, and I only remember Daddy going down there a few times. I think that's where he kept the wood for the pot-bellied stove.

We had two toilets—one for daytime use and one for nighttime use. The day toilet was a knotty-pine outhouse in the back yard. The night toilet was a white enamel pot with a lid that sat on the landing at the top of the stairs. If we'd had money, we would have called it a chamber pot. Since we didn't, we called it a slop jar. It was emptied every morning in the outhouse by one of the older kids.

Our bathtub was a galvanized tin tub, placed in the center of the kitchen. Mama hung a sheet for the older kids so they could have some privacy. We didn't have a hot water tank, so Mama heated water on the stove. Sometimes, three or four of us bathed in the same water before it was dumped. Baths usually started with Buster, the youngest. That was good for me because I was next in line and the water wasn't too dirty. And it was usually still very warm. The tub, along with a washboard, doubled as our washing machine.

My father, Isaac, was a laborer and a janitor, who had moved to Dayton from Louisiana. He never finished school. He was self-educated and eventually became a 32° Mason. My mother, Ellen, was also from Louisiana and worked as a cook when she wasn't pregnant.

I shared a double bed with my sisters, Betty and Dean. Also in our room were a baby bed, in which Buster slept, and a set of bunk beds. Ben and Ed shared one of the beds; Bob and Bill shared the other. Lewis, the oldest, slept on a rollaway bed downstairs. My oldest sister, Corine, was the only child from my father's first marriage. She lived in Louisiana with her mother. Of the ten children my parents had together, I was number eight.

Occasionally, in the summer, we'd sleep outside. Mama and Daddy would make a large pallet of newspaper and blankets, and we'd sleep in the front yard under the stars. When the wind was just right, we could smell the flowers, peaches and pears as we drifted off to sleep.

The potbelly was in the middle room, and didn't generate enough heat to warm the whole house. In the winter, my brothers stuffed newspapers around the windows and hung heavy quilts to keep the wind out. I slept between my sisters, so I was usually pretty warm.

Generally, we were happy, at least I thought we were. There were some minor problems, especially with the older boys, but overall, we were happy. Despite whatever frustrations and challenges they may have faced, my parents provided a good home for us. I remember birthday parties, dolls and clothes at Christmas, new clothes and shoes at Easter. I vaguely remember going to Lakeside Amusement Park on "colored day". And I loved our Saturday excursions to the Regal Theatre. We'd stop at Sylvia's Market to buy penny candy. My favorites were banana KITS, Mary Janes, and Necco Wafers. Then we'd head out for an afternoon of movies.

Going to the movies was fun, but the best part was riding high above everybody on the street from my lofty perch on Lewis' shoulders. How I loved Lewis. I loved all my brothers and sisters, but there was just something about Lewis. He was so tall and so handsome. And he had the prettiest smile. He was ten years and three months older than I was. And to me, that seemed like a lifetime.

As far as I was concerned, Lewis could do no wrong. Even when he was wrong, he was right with me. I suppose every little girl, at one time or another, feels that way about her big brother.

Daddy was in the Elks and I remember their picnics and parades. No man, anywhere, ever looked as good as my daddy when he dressed for the Elks' parades. He put on his off-white pants, shirt, gloves, and shoes, and his burgundy fez and sash. I could spot him a mile away. At nearly 6'3", he was one of the tallest in his lodge. His height and his rich, coffee-colored skin made him stand out from the rest. The other men appeared so ordinary marching beside my daddy. His long, lean frame seemed to glide through the streets as if he were walking on air. People from all over the colored side of town would come out to watch the Elks' parades. And when my daddy strutted and high-stepped in those parades, I thought that somehow his stature rubbed off on me and I was so much more important than I would otherwise be.

◇

Buster wasn't in school yet, and I only went for half a day. We had so much fun playing together. Sometimes we just sat on the ground and played in the dirt or made mud pies. Sometimes we played Dragnet, and when we played house, Mama would give us a little of whatever she was cooking so I could feed "my husband" when he came home from work. But our favorite thing was to sit on the kitchen floor and watch Mama cook. We loved watching her mix cake batter. Mama was short, about 4'10", and heavy. She'd balance the bowl on her left hip and whip the batter with a long, wooden spoon gripped tightly in her right hand. The flab on her upper arm flapped like a flag in the breeze. We thought that was the funniest thing. We tried to get our arms to jiggle like that, but our efforts were in vain.

Mama had a cure for everything. A chunk of Argo starch was the cure for diarrhea and vomiting. Castor Oil was the cure for constipation. Cod Liver Oil and Vick's Salve were the cures for colds. And a blue popsicle was the cure for everything else.

Popsicles and Barq's Creme of Soda were staples in our house. It was Dean who was responsible for the blue popsicles, though. I don't remember when it happened; I was probably just a toddler. Mama usually took Betty and Dean to the market. As they walked by the ice-cream freezer one day, Mama asked what color popsicle they wanted. Dean piped up, "I want a blue one."

Mama said, "They don't make blue popsicles."

Dean, feeling a bit dejected, chose another color and walked home in silence. After that, every time she went to the Sylvia's Market, Dean walked by the freezer and looked for blue popsicles. And one day, she saw them. She grabbed one and shrieked, "Mama look! A blue popsicle!" And that's how the trend got started. If none of her home remedies seemed appropriate, Mama gave us blue popsicles to quiet us down until she could figure out what to do. When Bill fell on a coffee can and cut his side, he carried on something awful. Mama gave him a blue popsicle to calm him down so they could get him to the doctor's office. When I stepped on a rusty nail, she gave me a blue popsicle to divert my attention from my foot. It didn't do a thing for the bleeding, but it surely stopped me from crying.

As far as I knew, everybody lived like we did. We didn't have a lot, but we didn't do without either. If we did, I didn't know about it. I was, for the most part, a shy but happy child. All of that changed on a cold day in January 1956, when our world was turned upside down. None of us would ever be the same.

# Chapter 2

༄

I t was January 15th. It had been snowing for a few days and it was so cold. Mama was in labor with her 10th child. My sisters and I helped her get dressed. Well, with the exception of buttoning the last two buttons on the front of her dress, I basically watched. I couldn't quite grasp the concept of a baby growing inside my mother. I didn't have a clue about where babies came from and I really didn't think there was one inside my mother. But I knew that something was in there, and it was making Mama's stomach hurt. It had to come out. She was in so much pain, and that thing, whatever it was, was moving. A lot!

Mama got her coat and we went downstairs. The boys were just waiting around downstairs and Daddy was standing in the doorway between the front room and the middle room. The cab pulled up and Mama kissed us good-bye. "I'll be home soon," she said. Daddy told us to mind Lewis and Betty and that he'd see us 'directly.' Since the big kids had taken over the downstairs windows and the front door, Buster and I ran to the upstairs window. We waved for a long time as the cab inched down the snow-covered street. We continued to wave long after the cab was out of sight.

We gathered in the middle room and huddled around the potbelly. An eerie silence hung over the room. I don't know how I knew, but I knew that she wasn't coming back. I don't know if anyone else knew it or not. Sitting there, amid eight brothers and sisters, I felt so alone. I began to cry. "Ya'll, Mama ain't comin' back."

Lewis and Betty tried to assure me that she'd be home in a few days. They had been through this before, many times before. I didn't believe them. As the oldest—Lewis, who had just turned sixteen, and Betty, who was twelve—they were just doing their jobs, trying to take care of us. That meant doing the right thing and saying the right thing, whether they believed it or not. We waited anxiously for Daddy to call from the hospital. The phone didn't ring.

Some time later, there was a knock at the front door. It was Miss Jenkins. She was a nurse and had been involved with our family for years. I didn't remember seeing her before, but Betty said I had, so I had to believe that. And though we knew she was married, we always called her Miss Jenkins. When she came to the house that day, she still had on her uniform and hat and a camel-tan overcoat. She was an imposing figure, tall—about 5'7", and wore silver cat-eye glasses that sat high on her long, narrow nose. She had a direct, almost gruff way about her. When she spoke, she meant business. She told the boys to mind Lewis and not to start any foolishness. She took Buster by the hand and said, "Girls, you and Walter will stay with me tonight. Get your coats. Get Walter's coat too." I really didn't want to go, but I knew I dared not say so. So, reluctantly, I put on my coat and we got into her car.

Her house was so much different from ours. It was big, with a big porch and a swing. There were two doors off the front porch; one opened into the living room and the other opened into a large bedroom. When we walked in, the first thing I noticed was the piano—in the living room! I didn't know people had pianos in their houses. I thought pianos belonged only in church or in school.

The kitchen was large enough to eat in, and there was a dining room too. Off the dining room was a smaller room that eventually became another bedroom for two of my brothers. Upstairs were two large bedrooms, and best of all was a full bathroom with a sink, a real tub, and a toilet! Off the bathroom was a smaller bedroom, actually a converted attic. And there were lights and lamps everywhere. I couldn't believe how big and bright that house was. For the first time, I began to realize that everybody didn't live like we lived. I decided at that moment that when I grew up, I would become a nurse, just like Miss Jenkins, *cause nurses are rich!*

There were four Jenkins children: three girls, Barbara, Joan, and Derry, and a boy, Terran. Joan, the middle daughter, took an immediate liking to me. She had strong mothering instincts, and since her younger siblings were getting too big, she didn't have many opportunities to mother anyone until I came along. That night was the first time I remember bathing in a real bathtub. Joan gave me a bubble bath and sprinkled talcum powder all over me, and told me I could sleep with her—just the two of us, alone in her big bed. I felt so good that I actually forgot why we were there.

The next day, we awoke to a big breakfast of bacon, scrambled eggs, grits, sweet rolls, orange juice, and milk. Miss Jenkins was already dressed for work when we went downstairs. Mr. Jenkins had already gone to work. She told us to behave, and said that a sitter was coming over to stay with Buster and me. She told Joan and Barbara to "do something" with our hair and make sure we had clean clothes to put on, then she left.

I don't remember going to school that day. Buster and I had so much fun in that great big house. There were so many places to hide. My fascination with the bathtub was matched only by Buster's. We played in the tub. We didn't fill it and play in the water; we just played in the empty tub. We wore ourselves out, going from room to room. Around mid-day, the sitter made us take a nap. Though we balked at first, we were sleeping soundly within a matter of minutes. Shortly after we awoke, everybody was coming home from school. My brothers came over too. I couldn't wait to show them the tub, and the inside toilet, and all the beds. We had a big dinner, and scattered throughout the house, playing, talking, and watching television.

The following day was much the same. The boys came over after school and we all ate dinner together. We dispersed throughout the house doing whatever we had a mind to do. I don't remember what time it was; I just know that it was dark. For some reason, my mind is set at 7:30. Anyway, Miss Jenkins called us into the living room. Daddy was sitting in the chair, a red chair by the front door. His legs were spread and his elbows rested on his knees. His hands were clasped tightly together, and he stared at the floor. He didn't look up when we came in, and he didn't respond when we spoke. He just sat there, staring at the floor. We all sat down and waited.

Finally, after what seemed an eternity, he said, without looking up, "Well, Ellen didn't make it." I started to ask, "Didn't make what?" But Betty's screams shattered the silence. She ran upstairs. Dean, also in tears, followed close behind. I just sat there, not knowing what was happening and not knowing what to do. Buster was more confused than I was. Lewis walked outside with tears streaming down his face. Ben sat in the chair crying. Bob, Ed, and Bill just sat expressionless, and Daddy just stared at the floor.

I wanted somebody to tell me what was going on. *What was Mama suppose to make? Why couldn't she make it? Why is everybody crying? Why won't Daddy look at us? Why is he so sad?* I ran upstairs to join my sisters. They were sitting on the bed, hugging and crying. I started crying too, not because I understood what was happening, but simply because they were.

The next day, Betty explained it to me the best way she could. She said Mama got sick when the baby was being born. The baby, another boy, was fine. His name was Daved, but Daddy called him Tiny. Mama had something called toxemia and it made her blood pressure go up. The doctor couldn't get her pressure down and she started bleeding in her brain. Betty said that when your brain bleeds, you die.

She said, "We'll never see her again. But she can still see us. And she'll always be with us. In fact, she's probably sitting on the bed beside us right now."

I scooted close to Betty to make sure there was enough room for Mama on the bed. I kept looking at the empty space, thinking that I'd see the bed cave in where she was sitting. Betty put her arm around me and said, "You can talk to her if you want. She can hear you, but you can't hear her."

I whispered, "Hi, Mama." As usual, Betty was right. If Mama answered me, I didn't hear her.

Miss Jenkins was very decisive and had a "take charge" attitude. I don't know whose decision it was, but somebody decided that the four younger boys and I would ride to the funeral with Miss Jenkins and Terran, rather than with the rest of the family. We went by our house first and had prayer with Daddy, the minister, and the funeral directors. Uncle Willie had come up from Louisiana. I hadn't seen him since I was three, when Mama took Buster and me to her mother's funeral. I didn't remember Uncle Willie. He remembered me, though. I kept looking at him, trying to find something, anything that would make me remember him, but I didn't.

When we got to the funeral home, Miss Jenkins parked the car. Buster asked her what dead meant. She turned to us and said, "It's sort of like your mother is asleep." Well, that was certainly good to know. I still wasn't sure what dead meant, except that it made Betty scream, it made my brothers cry, and it made my daddy sad. But I knew what sleep meant. I also knew that Mama was ticklish behind her ears. If I tickled her, she would wake up.

We went inside. Everybody else was already there. Daddy was off to the side, sitting alone near the front door, staring at the floor. I ran to him. His eyes were red. My daddy had been crying! I grabbed his neck and hugged him. "Don't cry, Daddy." He picked me up as he stood. He didn't say anything. He just hugged me and kissed my cheek. When he put me down, I walked over to the casket. Buster was already standing there, trying to get a closer look. He was so little at three years old that he could barely see into the casket. He whispered to her, "Mama. Mama, you thleep?" She didn't respond. I tickled her behind her right ear and called her. "Mama. Mama, it's me." She didn't respond to me either. Something wasn't right. She didn't look right. *Why is her skin so cold and so hard? Why does it look gray, instead of her usual caramel brown? Why won't she answer me?* I grabbed Buster's hand and we ran to Daddy. "Daddy, Mama won't wake up."

Daddy sat and put Buster on his lap. Lewis picked me up and walked toward the door.

Lewis struggled to find the words. "Baby, Mama ain't gonna' never wake up. She's dead."

"But Miss Jenkins said she was just sleep," I argued.

" 'Member that duck we had that died, and we put it in a box and buried it out back, 'cross the alley?"

"Yea."

"Well," he said. "That's what they're going to do with Mama. She's dead, just like that duck. And they're going to bury her."

"Out back 'cross the alley?" I wanted to know.

"No, in the cemetery."

"What's a cemetery, Lewis?"

"It's a graveyard." He could tell by looking at me that I didn't know anymore about graveyards than I did about cemeteries. He tried again. "It's a place where they bury dead people. There's lots of people buried there."

"Then how will we know which one is Mama?"

He hesitated for a moment, then said, "They put big rocks on the graves with the dead peoples names on them."

"We goin' to the graveyard?"

"You can't go. Miss Jenkins said you too little."

"But I wanna' go."

"No, you can't go!" He was getting agitated.

Miss Jenkins had rounded up the younger boys, and as she neared the door, she signaled to Lewis that it was time for me to go. He put me on the floor, patted my head, and said, "See ya' later, alligator." Miss Jenkins ushered us out the door and into her car. After she started the car, I asked, "Miss Jenkins, we goin' to the cemetery?"

"No, I don't think you need to do that. Your father and I talked about it."

"But I wanna' go."

"You're not going. You're too young."

I certainly didn't understand that. When I went on the train to Louisiana with Mama, I was only three years old. I went to her mother's funeral. I stayed for the whole thing. And Buster and I went to the cemetery. I just didn't know that's what it was called. I watched the minister throw a handful of dirt on the casket and everything. And I saw people throw flowers in the hole on top of the casket. *If Mama didn't think I was too young to go to a cemetery at three, why does Daddy think I'm too young at five? I didn't know Mama's mother. But I knew my mother. Why doesn't anybody think it's important for me to go to the cemetery? Why didn't somebody ask me what I want to do?* I was mad at Miss Jenkins. I just knew it was her idea for us not to go. She

13

was so bossy.

When we got to the house, there was food everywhere. We weren't gone long enough for anyone to cook all of that. I wondered where it came from. There were some women in the kitchen. I don't know who they were. Miss Jenkins told us she had work to do and that we should go upstairs and watch television.

I don't know how long we'd been there, probably close to two hours, when we heard voices, a lot of voices, coming from downstairs. Miss Jenkins called us downstairs to eat. The funeral, the trip to the cemetery, everything was over. Buster and I started downstairs first, followed by Ed, Bob, Bill and Terran. I wondered who all those people were. I wandered through the crowd and into the kitchen, dragging Buster behind me. I couldn't believe my eyes. There was already a lot of food when we went upstairs, but somehow, the food had multiplied by at least three or four times. There were hams, fried chicken, baked chicken, roast beef, yams, mashed potatoes, potato salad, macaroni and cheese, cabbage, greens and green beans, black-eyed peas and rice, cornbread and rolls, and every kind of dessert I could imagine. There was almost as much food in that house as there was at the Elk's picnics. It was like a big party. Everybody ate and talked and laughed and had a good time—everybody except Daddy. He sat in the red chair by the front door and stared at the floor.

Buster walked over to him and offered him a bite of the chicken leg he carried in his hand. Daddy just shook his head. Buster climbed up on his lap and hugged him. Daddy clung to Buster and rocked back and forth. That was the first time Daddy had moved since he walked into the house. He didn't say anything; he just rocked. Buster finally climbed down and went back into the kitchen.

I wanted to know who all those people were. I knew some of them from Paisley Street, Miss Dorothy and her husband,

Miss Zachary, the Scrivens, and the Glaspers. And the Fosters and a lot of the Elks were there with their wives, and Uncle Willie. I just walked around and looked at people, and listened to conversations I didn't understand. They left in groups of three or four, and as soon as one group left, it seemed that another group came. It went on for hours. Around 7:00, Miss Jenkins told Buster and me to go upstairs with Joan so she could give us our baths. "After you get your pajamas on, come say goodnight to your father. Willard, Robert and Edward, you go next."

We went upstairs and hopped in the tub, this time to bathe. When we came back downstairs, Daddy was still sitting in the red chair by the door. I felt sorry for him. He looked so sad. I had never seen Daddy look like that before. And it seemed that no matter who said or did what, nothing could make him smile. Not even Buster. We walked over and said, "Good night, Daddy." He hugged us and kissed us, but he didn't say anything. He didn't even tell us to be good or that he'd see us directly. I don't know how long Daddy sat in that chair, staring at the floor. I just know that when we got up the next morning, the chair was empty.

# Chapter 3

᪥

The girls and Buster were to stay with Miss Jenkins for a while. Somehow, almost all of us ended up there. The Browns, a childless couple, adopted Daved. I think Miss Jenkins knew them through some friends. They brought him over once, when he was just a few months old. Daddy was there. He held Tiny for a while, and talked to him and played with him. He had a strange look on his face when he handed him back to Mr. Brown. I don't remember if that was before or after the adoption was final. Whatever the case, I don't remember seeing Daved again. I thought about him a lot and wondered what happened to him. I wasn't sure if I'd ever see him again.

There was turmoil in the Jenkins house, and understandably so. The house that was once home to six people, was now home to thirteen. Lewis and Ben came over occasionally, but rarely stayed more than a day or two. The Jenkins girls seemed to fuss a lot. Joan pretty much became my defender against everybody except her mother.

I was a quiet, shy child. I didn't have a lot to say. If I talked, it was barely more than a whisper, except when I played with

Buster. Miss Jenkins was constantly yelling at me to stand up straight or to speak up. I didn't understand why she was so adamant about me talking. If I'd had something to say, I would have said it. That, as far as I was concerned, was a major problem with a lot of people. They talked all the time, and didn't really say much of anything. I rarely talked to anyone except Buster. He was my pal. The boys didn't want him tagging along because he would slow them down. Betty and Dean didn't want me hanging around them most of the time. There was a natural division among the Gibson kids anyway. Lewis and Ben were born two years apart and they were always together. Betty and Dean were a year apart. They were always together. The middle boys, Bill, Bob, and Ed, were all born in July with one year separating one from the next, so they were always together. Buster was two years younger than I was, so we were always together. It's a good thing we really liked each other. Besides, Buster's lisp was so bad I was about the only person who could understand him.

Near the end of March, I was particularly sad. My birthday was coming and my mother wasn't around to celebrate with me. I guess Miss Jenkins sensed what I was going through. She picked me up after school one day and took me shopping for a new winter coat. We looked and looked, but it seemed that what I liked she didn't; and fortunately, what she liked didn't fit. She said we would look for a few more minutes, and if she didn't find one, we'd go home and shop somewhere else another time. As we headed toward the front door, something caught her eye. "Oh, look at this," she said. I was half-afraid to, but I did. And to my surprise, it was the most beautiful coat I had ever seen— a sky blue car coat with a hood. The hood and sleeves were trimmed with white fake fur. The quilted lining was bright yellow. I didn't want to try it on for fear that it wouldn't fit. "Here," she said. "Try this on."

I slowly took off my coat and put on the new one. "Let me see. Turn around. Hold your arms out in front of you. Hold your hands up. Way up." She looked at the price tag. "Take it off. Let's get this coat and go home."

We went to the register to pay for the coat. She put the change in her purse and asked me if I wanted to carry the bag. Of course I did. We got in her car and I thanked her over and over gain. I kept looking in the bag and thinking, *This is really my coat! This is really my coat!* I couldn't wait to show Buster. I couldn't wait for Betty and Dean to come home from school so I could show them. Miss Jenkins had already bought me a dress and a pair of black patent leather shoes. They were very nice, mind you, but this coat, well, it was the best thing ever! I could hardly play with Buster for trying on my coat. I didn't feel ordinary anymore. In that coat, I was the most beautiful girl in the world.

Joan made my birthday even more special. The Saturday after my birthday, we had a tea party. It was a private affair. Only four of us were present; Joan, a worn brown Teddy bear, a big white doll, and I. Joan dressed me in one of her old dresses and we put on high heels, hats and gloves. She even put hats on the bear and the doll. We sat at a small table in the bedroom. We drank red Kool-Aid from little white teacups with pink flowers, and ate cheese curls and caramel popcorn off the little matching plates. We sat and chatted like we were rich, famous women who lived in big houses with servants. We had a wonderful time. At first, I wanted Buster to be at the party, but after a while, I forgot all about him. I was so caught up in the fantasy that I forgot about everything and everybody else.

◇

I don't know how or when my father found out about the orphanage in Xenia. Daddy knew he couldn't provide for us the way he would have liked. He had been told that, at the Home, we would all be together. We would attend one of the best schools in the state. There was a trade school and we all would learn the trade of our choice. And there was a hospital on campus if we needed medical attention. There were planned activities on the weekends and we'd go to camp in the summer. They would feed us, clothe us, and tend to our every need.

The Ohio Soldiers' and Sailors' Orphans' Home was built in the 1860s for children orphaned by the Civil War. Later, the rules admitted any child if at least one parent had served in the military. Since Daddy served in the Army during the World War I, we met the eligibility criteria. So, on July 2, 1956, we were uprooted and sent somewhere else to live. Once again, our world would be turned upside down.

That morning, Miss Hacker, a social worker, arrived early in her station wagon to pick us up. Lewis didn't go. He was too old at 16, plus he had been in some minor scrapes with the law and was considered incorrigible by the Home's standards. Miss Jenkins had sent her son, Terran to spend the summer with his grandfather in Alabama and Ed had gone with him. The rest of us loaded our things in the car. Daddy kissed us good-bye and told us to be good. "I'll come see you as much as I can," he said.

We piled into the car and headed to the Home. I looked back at my father. He had that look on his face again; the one he had when he told us that Mama died. As the car pulled away, he stood in the street with his hand in the air, until the car was out of sight. He didn't wave; he just held his hand in the air.

The silence in the car was broken only by muffled sniffles. Nobody said anything for a long time. Buster looked at Ben and said, "Don't cry Ben, hear?" At that point, we all started to cry. There was something quite touching about four-year-old Buster telling his fourteen-year-old brother not to cry, especially since crying was what we all wanted to do. The social worker tried to ease our anxiety. She talked about all the things the Home had to offer.

"We have football and basketball and track teams. We've won regional and state championships, you know. I'll show you some of the trophies if you like. And you girls will learn to cook and sew and type. Won't that be fun? And you'll get to go swimming and go to dances. You'll see. You'll like it at OSSO."

It was only about 18 miles away, but the trip seemed to take forever. Finally she said, "Well children, we're here."

The main entrance was ominous; down right scary. On each side of the driveway was a gray stone column, about seven feet high, topped with a brass cannon. I remembered the westerns we saw at the Regal Theater and how the cowboys shot cannons at the Indians. I remembered that six or seven Indians would fly through the air for each cannonball the cowboys fired. *If we try to leave, will they shoot those cannons at us? If we all leave together, one cannonball would kill all seven of us.*

As she turned the car into the long driveway, she started pointing to various buildings. On the right was the chapel, with a small cemetery behind it. I wondered if Mama was buried there. The gym was close to the chapel, with a small grove of pear trees in between. "That's where you'll play basketball, and volleyball, and jump on the trampoline. And there's a swimming pool downstairs." She tried so hard to make it sound exciting.

Next to the gym was a large auditorium with giant pillars gracing the top of the steps. "We show movies there on Saturdays and put on plays. We have a drama department, you know." I wanted to yell at her, *No, we don't know. How would we know that? Besides, I don't even know what a drama department is.*

She continued, "The Orphan's Den is in there too. Dances and week-end socials are held in the Den." Next to that was the school. We couldn't really see the buildings all that well.

She was driving one way, and we were looking the other. "But," she said, "you'll have plenty of time to get to know the campus."

She kept driving up the winding road. We rode past the band shell where they had outdoor concerts. "You'll have music lessons too," she said. "You can pick any instrument you want. Maybe some of you will play in the band. Wouldn't you like that?" No one answered. Across from the band shell was the parade field. It was big, and the outer edge was ringed with the biggest trees I had ever seen.

"You boys will be in the ROTC Program. You'll take classes in military science and you'll learn drills. On Sundays, you'll get to march in the parades with the marching band. It's so patriotic."

On the other side of the parade field were several identical buildings. They were long, red brick, two-story houses with two front doors, two sets of steps and a verandah on each end. She called them cottages and started naming them. I didn't remember the names, though. I just remember her saying they were named after former US presidents.

The main building sat high off the ground with a front porch that overlooked a fountain in the middle of the square. Attached to the back of the building was the teachers' cafeteria. The children's main dining room was attached to that. Behind the dining room was the armory. That stretch of buildings represented the dividing line, which separated the boys' side of the campus from the girls'. We would learn later that there were lines, in just about every facet of Home life, that separated us, in one form or another.

We passed the powerhouse, football field, the track and the Superintendent's house and finally arrived at the hospital. Standard procedure was that new arrivals stayed in quarantine for two weeks for physicals, immunizations, and psychological evaluations.

When we walked in, three nurses met us in the waiting

room. Two were sitting. I had a feeling that the one who was standing was the boss nurse. She was the first to speak. She was tall, taller than Miss Jenkins. Her name was Mrs. Neville. Her graying hair was pulled back in a bun and she wore silver cat eyes. She had a long, narrow nose with a slight hump at the bridge. Her eyes were blue and so clear. I had seen white people. In fact, there was a white family who lived across the alley from us. But I don't remember them having eyes like hers.

As she spoke, I stared at her mouth. Her lips were so small. She barely had a top lip at all. I couldn't concentrate on what she said. I was too busy watching her mouth. The way she talked reminded me of Miss Jenkins. They didn't sound alike or anything like that. She just talked like she meant business. It didn't take long to figure out that she was the boss nurse. I had already decided I wanted to be a nurse. Now I wanted to be tall, like Mrs. Neville and Miss Jenkins so I could be the boss nurse. I didn't really know if Miss Jenkins was a boss nurse or not; I just knew she was bossy.

One nurse took the girls to a room; the other took the boys. Our rooms were at the far end of the hospital, closest to the cottages, and away from the clinic and the patients. We were given a brief tour of our quarters. The walls were pale green, with bright pictures of all the characters from Snow White painted at the top as a border. The room was large enough to accommodate four beds, four night stands, and a dining table with four chairs. The adjoining bathroom had a sink, toilet, tub, and two shower stalls. I was amazed—a tub and two showers! *Man, they must really be rich here. This bathroom is better than the one at Miss Jenkins' house.*

"This will be your room for the next two weeks," she said. "You are not to leave this room unless given permission. You may have a radio upon request, but no television. And if the radio is too loud, it will be taken away and you will lose that privilege. Pick a bed and get settled. It's time for your nap." With that, she left.

We picked our beds and got ready for our nap. The beds were so high that I needed to use a chair to get in mine. My bed. My very own bed. I didn't have to share it with anybody. I hadn't slept alone since Buster was born four years ago and took over the crib.

As soon as I settled down, I noticed her, staring at me. Her long stringy gray hair was sticking out from under her black hat. Her beady black eyes were filled with evil and her mouth was curled into a wicked sneer. She had a big hooked nose with a wart on the end. I hadn't noticed her before. I was afraid of her, the witch from Snow White painted on the wall right above Dean's bed.

"Betty, that witch keeps looking at me."

"She can't hurt you. It's just a painting."

"But I can't take no nap with her up there. She's gonna get me. I'm scared."

Betty told Dean to trade beds with me, but it didn't help. No matter where I went, the witch was scowling at me. I tried resting on my stomach, but that didn't help either. I couldn't see her at all then, and I wouldn't know if she somehow magically came to life and was coming to get me. I needed to be in a position to see her. At least if I saw her coming, I'd have a fair chance to get away.

When the nurse came to check on us, Betty told her that we needed to move to another room. "My little sister doesn't want to sleep in here. She's scared of the witch."

The reply was immediate and crisp. "Children don't make the decisions here at OSSO. It doesn't matter what she wants. She'll just have to get used to it." I had a feeling, right then, that I was not going to like this place.

◇

We didn't get to see the boys much, except when we went out to play. Their rooms were about three doors from ours and on the other side of the hall. Occasionally, we'd all be in the clinic together, getting shots or getting exams but we couldn't visit each other's rooms.

There was a small play area behind the hospital that had a sliding board, some rings, and three swings. In the distance, we could see the kids playing and having a good time. They were all little kids, about my age and Buster's age, and they were all white. And there were three play grounds; one for the boys, which was closest to the hospital; one for the girls; and one across the creek. The boys' playground had a merry-go-round, a sandbox, a jungle gym, monkey bars, two swing sets, three teeter-totters, and a sliding board. The girls' side had a swing set, a jungle-gym, monkey bars, and teeter-totters. And across the creek were monkey bars, a high bar, a jungle gym, and swings. No one played across the creek though.

I wanted to get a closer look at those kids. All the boys had the same haircut, a burr, like military men. And most of the girls had hair like the little boy on the Dutch Boy paint can, just in different colors. A few of them had ponytails. Some of them waved to us. We waved back and smiled, but we dared not venture too close. We had been told not to go beyond the boundary line at the edge of the hospital. I didn't want to find out what would happen if we did.

I could see part of the farm from the hospital playground. The cows were out grazing, and I could see a couple of workhorses. I wondered what other kinds of animals they had. I hadn't seen many farm animals before, just dogs, ducks, and a few birds. When Mama took Buster and me to Louisiana, I did see a pig. But never had I seen a cow or a horse. I thought, *This might not be so bad after all.*

◇

By this time, everybody had heard about us. We were a bit of a novelty. Most of the kids came to the home in groups of two or three, occasionally four or five; but never seven from one family at one time. We'd had all our shots and tests and the two weeks passed quickly. We were "going down", which meant we were going to our cottage. I was anxious to see what the inside of our cottage looked like. I still thought we'd all be together, in one cottage.

When we left the hospital, the boys were led in one direction and Betty, Dean and I were led in another. We went to Taft B, the colored girls' cottage. I didn't know where my brothers were.

The walk to the cottage was an adventure. There was so much to see and so many people wanted to see us. We could see girls peeking out of windows and supervisors standing in doorways. As we reached the main campus, we could hear the white girls talking. Some spoke, some didn't. Someone whispered, "Those are the newkies." I didn't know what "newkie" meant. I learned later that it was Orphan slang for new kids.

Our supervisor was Mrs. Vincent. She was the only full-time colored supervisor on the girls' side. When we got to the cottage, all the girls came down to meet us. They wanted to know everything about us. "Where are you from?" "How old are you?" "Are there really seven of you guys?" "I heard your mother had ten kids." "Where are the rest of your brothers and sisters?" The questions came fast, often two or three at a time. I didn't like that. They were nice enough, but it was just too much, too fast, from too many strangers.

We shared the big room on the first floor. We settled in and Betty and Dean chose beds. Betty took the single bed. Dean took the bottom bunk. There was one bed and one sister left, so guess who get stuck with the top bunk

There were two other bedrooms downstairs, plus the supervisor's quarters. The bathroom had a toilet, sink, and shower. There was a heavy green metal door at the end of the hall near the bathroom. Upstairs were six bedrooms and another bathroom that had two toilets, a tub, and three sinks. There was a heavy green metal door upstairs too. The verandah looked like a good place to sit in the summer, especially at night. We could get to it through a window in the hall or from the bedroom at the top of the stairs. But I learned, on the first day, that we were not allowed on the verandah.

The basement had two large laundry sinks, a couch, and several folding chairs. In the corner was a table with a hot plate and several straightening combs and curlers. That's where we did our hair, once a week on Saturday. There was a tan metal double door in the basement. Betty asked about the doors.

Mrs. Vincent answered, "You are not to go beyond those doors. There's another cottage over there. All of the cottages have doors like that. They separate the A side from the B side. Do not open those doors."

There was something about Mrs. Vincent that frightened me. She was so calm; too calm. It was as if she deliberately tried to keep herself from exploding all the time. She had served with the Women's Army Corps, and had perfect, ram-rod-straight posture, and expected the same from all of us. She was articulate and knew more words than anyone I'd ever heard before. She spoke slowly and deliberately, pronouncing every syllable and every letter of every word. She would not tolerate a mispronounced word. And there was no such thing as "I can't say it." She'd make us repeat it until we said it right, no matter how long it took. It was nerve wracking.

At dinner time, we lined up at the back door to go to the dining room. As we left the cottage, girls from the other cottages were filing out too. They kept looking at us. I was starting to get worried. I didn't see the boys. And I didn't see any of the little kids. All the girls were teenagers. There was one colored girl in our cottage the same age as Dean, who was almost eleven. Everybody else on campus was older than that. *What happened to all those little kids we saw from the hospital?* Betty put her arm around me. "What's the matter?"

"I thought I was gonna' get to play with those little kids,

27

but they're gone."

"Oh," she said, "they're probably still around."

"Where?"

"I don't know, but I'll find out."

We got to the dining room and took our seats. Everyone sat in cottage groups. The boys filed in through a door on the other side of the building. Dean was the first to notice a group of colored boys as they entered the dining room.

"Hey, Ben!" she shouted.

Mrs. Vincent told her to be quiet.

"But that's my big brother. I can talk to him if I want."

"No, you may not. We don't shout across the dining room here at OSSO. Now be quiet."

I looked across the room and saw Buster. He waved frantically. I felt a little better. I waved back. I saw all my brothers except Bill. There were more colored boys in the Home than there were colored girls. They had two cottages, Adams A and Adams B. There were three little colored boys, besides Buster; one was four, one was six, and one was seven. At least Buster had somebody to play with. *Where is Bill? How come he isn't he in the cottage with the rest of my brothers?*

There were about 400 kids in the dining room. Miss Connery was one of the dietitians. When she played the bells, everybody got quiet. That was the signal to say grace. After that, we had twenty minutes to eat. Some of the older girls wore aprons. They were on detail, which meant they went to the dining room early to set the tables, and stayed late to clean up. They would get up mid-way through the meal to serve dessert. Some supervisors allowed their kids to talk during meals, some didn't. Mrs. Vincent let us talk, but in very low tones. The boys generally talked louder, in more normal tones.

When we left the dining room, Dean asked Betty, "How come Bill wasn't in the dining room?"

Betty gave her usual reply. "I don't know, but I'm gonna' find out."

Betty was always going to find out something or other. Most of the time she did. I truly believed Betty could do anything. No matter what it was, Betty could find out. I knew she'd find out about Bill, too. I didn't know how she'd do it, but I knew that she would.

After we ate, we left the dining room in cottage groups. We changed clothes and went outside to play. The playground was a lot bigger than the one I'd seen from the hospital. This one had two sets of swings, a sliding board, and four teeter-totters. It also had a volleyball court and a softball diamond. There was a square bounded by Monroe, Taft, and Jackson. There was no equipment in the square, though. That was mostly for talking and reading. Hayes Hall was a cottage for senior girls and it was the only cottage on that side of the walk. It sat up on a hill and had large columns in front and a big side porch. None of the other cottages looked like that. Garfield and Jefferson were on the other end, close to the dining room. Directly across from the dining room was a brick building with no windows. The door was padlocked. I learned later that the bicycles, roller skates, and other playground equipment were stored there. I don't know how many of each, but it wasn't unusual to see thirty or forty girls riding bikes at the same time.

All of the children were assigned to cottages by age, except the colored kids. We were all housed together. Being on campus made me a bit of a novelty, since I was the only girl my age on campus. In a way, I was everybody's baby. Many of the girls, especially the white girls, felt an overwhelming need to look out for me, even if I didn't need looking out after. But I relished the attention. It made me feel special.

Saturdays were special too. It was hair day, and it was like a big party, only without dancing and food. Most of us would congregate in the basement all day. Some girls did their own hair, while some had others do theirs for them. Occasionally, Millie or Bonita did mine, but most of the time, Betty did it. They talked about everything: cute boys; whether Jackie Wilson could out-sing or out-perform Johnny Mathis; whether Nancy Wilson was more beautiful than Diahann Carroll. Half the time, I didn't know what they were talking about, but it didn't really matter. We had fun.

◇

I didn't go to camp that summer, but going to the pool was exciting. I couldn't swim at all, I enjoyed playing in the water. The white girls fussed over me and literally called 'next' to carry me around the pool. We also had gym in the afternoons. I didn't care too much for that. I was too small for most of the activities: basketball, softball, and volleyball. The trampoline looked like so much fun; but I couldn't see myself jumping up and down on an open-weave mat, suspended by springs. It just didn't look safe to me.

Life on the main campus wasn't so bad. Mrs. Vincent treated us pretty well, better than most supervisors treated their girls. We watched about two hours of television in the evenings. Sometimes, she'd let us stay up until 9:30 or 10:00, but generally, she followed the rule: in bed with lights out by 9:00. And in case we forgot, the powerhouse whistle went off at 9:00 sharp.

Just about everything we did was regulated by the powerhouse whistle. We had heard it when we were in the hospital, but no one explained what it was. The whistle sounded when it was time to get up, time to go to the dining room to set the tables, time to go eat, time to go to school. All day long, from 6:20 in the morning until 9:00 at night, the whistle would sound at pre-set intervals to remind us of what we were to do or where we were to be.

We went to church every Sunday morning. As with everything else, we sat in cottage groups, boys on one side, girls on the other. Service was about an hour. Rev. Walters seemed nice enough, but he didn't have the excitement in his preaching like the preacher back home. I don't remember going to church every Sunday when we lived in Dayton, but whenever Mama took us, it was something! The preacher got riled up and started to sweat. He'd whip a white handkerchief from his pocket and wipe his face. Sometimes, he'd almost sing his sermon. And he'd repeat stuff. And he'd yell, "I don't believe ya'll heard me," then say whatever it was again.

And the congregation would go crazy. People would jump up and shout, "Tell the story, preacha'." And sometimes, people would fall out. They'd be dancing and shouting in the aisles and boom, somebody, usually a woman, would hit the floor. The ushers or nurses—I was never sure which they were since they wore all white—would rush over and pull her dress down and cover her with a sheet. They'd stand over her and wave paper fans and whisper, "Thank you, Jesus."

We didn't have any of that at the Home. We sang a hymn. Rev. Walters prayed. The choir sang. Rev. Walters preached as if he'd rather be somewhere else doing something else. He was nice enough, but as a preacher, he just wasn't exciting. They passed the plate, and we went back to our cottages. No shouting. No "Amens." No "Wells." And definitely no falling out.

Sunday lunches were a really big deal. The food was a little better than usual. If we had ice cream, cake, or pie for dessert, it was usually on Sundays. And instead of bread, we had homemade rolls. They were good, but nothing to write home about. I guess if the other kids had tasted Mama's cooking, they wouldn't have been all that excited either.

Miss Simons was the relief supervisor for the colored cottage. Whenever Mrs. Vincent had a day off, Miss Simons would stay with us. She was hooked on the stories. Of the three that aired in those days, her favorite was *Love of Life*. She was so caught up in the lives of Bruce and Vanessa

Sterling that I thought she knew them personally. It was a toss up between *Search for Tomorrow* and the *Guiding Light* as to which came next. The goings on of the Tates and the Bauers occupied equal shares of her conversations. Miss Simons was single, and occasionally her man friend, Mr. Dennis, would come visit her. When he did, he would usually try to spend a little time with us. Sometimes, he'd bring a big box of chocolates for us to share.

We had been in the Home about two months when Ed came, just in time for the start of school. He had just returned from Alabama. It was after that when I learned that Bill had stayed in the hospital for several weeks after we were assigned to our cottages. Bill had always been a little slow. If he were a child today, he would be in a special education class. But the Home didn't offer such classes. And he was blind in one eye and could barely read. Since he didn't meet the Home's intelligence standards, he was sent to Orient. It was several years later when I learned that Orient was the state institution for the mentally retarded. Thank goodness. I thought he had been sent to China!

# Chapter 4

꓿

I was excited about going to school and couldn't wait to meet my teacher. I wasn't quite sure how this was going to work though. I had seen only two school buildings; one was the academic building and the other was the vocational building where high school kids learned trades. But I was certain there had to be a third building somewhere—one for the colored kids.

My cottage was closer to the school than most of the other cottages, so on the first day of school, I was the first one in my classroom. As I walked down the hall, I noticed that all the teachers were standing beside the doors to their rooms. There wasn't a colored teacher in the bunch.

My teacher was Mrs. Mart. As I reached the door, she patted my shoulder and welcomed me to first grade. She had the prettiest silver hair. It was short, thick, and wavy. And she had a warm smile. I smiled at her and walked into the room. I sat in the first seat in the first row. James Whitaker was the next to come in. We had never met or had the chance to talk but I recognized him from the dining room.

He waved and whispered, "Hi. I know your baby brother.

He's in my cottage."

I waved back. "I know. Your big sister is in my cottage." I don't know why we whispered. Mrs. Mart didn't say we couldn't talk, but for some reason, neither of us thought we should speak out loud. Whispering just seemed like the right thing to do.

I heard footsteps in the hall; no talking, just a lot of footsteps. Mrs. Mart spoke. "Come on, children. Let's get in here and take our seats. We don't want to be late on the first day, do we? Just sit anywhere. We'll assign seats after everyone is settled."

And here they came, all those little white kids. There were so many of them, and so many different shades, from pasty white to almost caramel. Most of them smiled and waved, but all of them looked surprised.

As Mrs. Mart called the roll, she pointed to the desk where we were to sit. When she called my name, she pointed to the desk behind Brenda Sue Dawson. Brenda Sue didn't look like the other girls. Instead of that ugly Dutch Boy hair cut, her long blonde hair was set in two ponytails that spiraled down to her shoulders. And her dress was different too. It wasn't dull and drab like the clothes the rest of us wore. Her dress was new, and a soft pastel and she wore ribbons and socks to match. And she had on black patent leather shoes, not the black and white saddle oxfords we wore. The same was true with Lillie Yancey. Her dark brown ponytail was half way down her back. Her dress wasn't as pretty as Brenda's, but it was a lot nicer than ours. And she wore black patent leather shoes too, just like Brenda's. I wondered who they were and why they looked so different. I found out later that their fathers worked at the Home. They lived in houses on campus, but they were not Orphans.

After roll call, Mrs. Mart told us what she expected from us. "I am Mrs. Mart and that is what you will call me, *Mrs. Mart*, not *Miss* Mart. There will be no talking in class, except during the free break, and even then, you will talk quietly. You will have one break in the morning and one in the afternoon. During that time, you will go to the bathroom in groups of three. You will have three minutes to get there and back. There will be no talking in the hall. And once you get to the bathroom, keep your voices down. The sound carries and we don't want to disturb the other classes.

"You will not have homework every day, but when you do, I expect it to be neat, and I will collect it first thing in the morning on the day it is due. If you don't turn in your homework, you will get a big fat goose egg. I will take attendance every day. When I call your name, please say "Present."

"When I ask questions, raise your hands. Do not speak until I call your name. Once I have called a name, the rest of you may put your hands down, unless I repeat the question or ask a new question. Now let's begin our lesson."

She passed out our books and supplies and admonished us to keep our desks neat and tidy. The lessons were actually very easy. We started with the alphabet, which we already knew. I mean, what six-year-old hasn't heard *The Alphabet Song* a million times? Printing the letters was a little different though. Some of us already knew how to do that too, but a lot of us didn't.

We spent about an hour on that, then moved to reading. I'd had just about enough of Sally, Dick, Jane, and Spot when Mrs. Mart announced it was time for our bathroom break. She randomly picked three boys and three girls. "Now remember," she said, "no talking in the hall."

I was teamed with Lauren and Emma. Lauren had dark brown, wavy hair and a round, pie face. Her summer tan was peeling, so I couldn't really tell what her true complexion was. She was a little shorter than Emma and I, and was slightly plump. She was cute.

Emma, on the other hand, was unique. She wasn't cute like most little kids. She was pretty—grown-up pretty. And she didn't look like the other kids, but she didn't look like me either. She was dark, like I had always imagined an Indian would look. She had a narrow nose and very thin lips. Her hair was jet black and so shiny. It looked so soft. Lauren's hair didn't shine like that, and neither did the other girls'. I wondered what kind of grease she used on it that made it shine like that but didn't weight it down like Dixie Peach Pomade did mine.

As we walked down the hall, I thought of dozens of questions to ask them. If I didn't ask soon, I knew I would burst. As soon as the bathroom door closed, I asked, "Where did you come from? Where do you live?"

Lauren responded, "Pan 6."

"What is Pan 6?" I wanted to know.

"Our cottage," she replied, as if I were the dumbest person in the world.

Emma asked, "How come you ain't in Peter Pan?"

"What is Peter Pan?"

Lauren was annoyed by this time. She put her hands on her hips and said, "Where we live."

On the main campus, all the cottages were named after former presidents. I didn't understand this Pan business. The only Peter Pan I'd ever seen was in a movie. It was a woman dressed like a little boy, who flew around in green stockings and a green elf suit. "But what is it? Where is it? How did you get there?" I wanted to know more.

Emma responded, "Peter Pan is where we live. And our cottage is Pan 6. Where do you live?"

Not sure if Peter Pan was part of the Home, I said, "At the OSSO Home. Taft B."

They looked at each other, then at me. Lauren asked, "How come you live up there? How come you don't live in Peter Pan?" I didn't have an answer for that, but I figured I'd ask Betty.

We each finished our business and our break was over. We

had to high tail it down the hall.

When we got back to class, all I could think about was Peter Pan. There were all these children in Peter Pan who were my age. *Why didn't I live with them instead of with teenagers? And where was Peter Pan? Why didn't I see them in the dining room? Where did they eat?* I didn't see them in chapel either. *Do they have a chapel where they live? Is Peter Pan what I saw from the hospital playground?* I had so many questions. I could hardly wait for the lunch recess. I wanted to ask Betty about Peter Pan. She probably knew. But if she didn't, I was sure she would find out.

Finally, we broke for lunch. I ran to the cottage and waited for Betty. She had barely stepped through the doorway when I shouted, "Betty, what is Peter Pan?"

"You remember. We saw it on television back home. But he wasn't real though. 'Member? The little boy who didn't want to grow up, and his friend, Tinkerbell." I just looked at her. "He got in a fight with Captain Hook, and . . ."

"Not that Peter Pan. The other one, where the little kids live."

"You mean Never Never Land. Peter Pan was the boy who took the little kids to Never Never Land so they wouldn't grow up."

By this time, I was exasperated. "Oh, never mind!" When Dean came into the room, I asked her. Her response was no different from Betty's. I walked out of the room and stood at the steps to line up for the dining room. I was still puzzled by this whole notion of Peter Pan. I wondered about it all the way to the dining room. After we said grace, I couldn't hold it in any longer. "Miss Vincent, what is Peter Pan?"

"Peter Pan is where the little children stay."

"Well, everybody in my class lives in Peter Pan, except me and James Whitaker. How come we ain't in Peter Pan?"

"Why *aren't* we in Peter Pan," she corrected.

"OK. Why aren't we in Peter Pan?"

She looked up, not at me but off in the distance and said, "There's never been a colored child in Peter Pan."

"Oh," I whispered. I was quiet throughout the rest of lunch. There was so much I wanted to know about Peter Pan. *How many cottages are in Peter Pan? How many kids live there? Is Peter Pan part of the Home? How come they don't eat with us or go to chapel with us? Can they come play with me some time? Can I go play with them?* This was the most fascinating thing. I wasn't the least bit bothered by the fact that there had never been a colored child in Peter Pan. I was just relieved and so happy that somebody finally knew what I was talking about.

After lunch, we had about half an hour before we went back to school. I couldn't wait to go back. I spent most of that time talking with my sisters about my teacher and my new friends. When we got back to school, we worked on our numbers and colors. We had our bathroom break mid-way through the afternoon. But during the last twenty minutes of school, Mrs. Mart gave us a free break to do whatever we wanted. Barbara Larson came over to my desk. She said, "I can write my name, see?" She showed me a sheet of paper on which she had printed her name. "Can you write?" she asked.

"Yea, watch," I replied. I wrote my name. She was astounded.

She turned to the other kids and said, "Hey, you guys, she can write in *curtsy.*" They crowded around my desk, peeking over each other's shoulders. Emma was the first to speak. "Can you write my name?"

"Probably. How do you spell it?"

She spelled it for me. Her name was easy. It only had three letters, and one of them was used twice. When I finished, I handed the paper to her. Man, was she impressed. Writing Barbara was a little harder. I used a combination of the numbers 7 and 3 to make the capital B. The lower case B looked like an F, but I don't think Barbara minded at all.

We talked for a while, mostly about why James and I weren't in Peter Pan. I told them what Mrs. Vincent had told me. And their response was the same as mine—"Oh."

As the final bell rang, Emma asked, "Will you teach me to write?"

"Yea, if you want me to."

She smiled. "You can be my friend if you want to."

Mrs. Mart called for us to line up at the door. James and I were in the front of the line. As we stepped out into the hall, she pointed us toward the center door and said, "We'll see you tomorrow." I could hear the footsteps of the other children moving away from us, toward the other door. I turned to see where they were going. Emma turned at the same time. We smiled and waved at each other and continued our separate ways.

I couldn't wait for Daddy and Miss Jenkins to come visit again. I wanted to tell them about school and my teacher. And I wanted to tell them about Peter Pan and show them my new friend, Emma. School had turned out to be an exciting, wonderful adventure.

I liked school and I liked Mrs. Mart. She was a good teacher. She told everybody how smart I was. Miss Hughes taught second grade, and Mrs. Patrick taught third. Sometimes, they would come get me out of class. I would go to their classrooms, stand in front of their students, and spell something they missed, or answer a question they didn't know. Most of the time, I knew the answer, especially if it was a spelling question. And they would say, "See here? She is in the first grade and she knows the answer. Aren't you ashamed? You don't know as much as a first-grader." Then they'd give me a treat and make me sit at the desk in front of the class and eat.

I didn't like the way they used me to embarrass their students. And I didn't like eating snacks in front of the other kids. It was always something really grand, like chocolate-covered Graham crackers and juice, or almond windmill cookies and chocolate milk. It wasn't fair and I didn't like it. At my old school in Dayton, the teacher let us have candy or bubble gum sometimes, but only if we brought enough for everybody. These teachers at the Home had enough for everybody, but they chose not to share. I thought that was mean.

Aside from making me go with Miss Hughes and Mrs. Patrick, I liked Mrs. Mart. I think she really liked us. She would hug us when we answered something right, and tell us how smart we were. And sometimes, she'd hug us if we answered wrong and say, "That was a good try." She played music while we took our rest break. Sometimes it was kiddie music, and sometimes it was classical. We played arithmetic games and spelling games. Sometimes we'd make up stories. We had a lot of fun in her class.

The weekends were hard for me. The only time I got to see my classmates was in school. I learned from Mrs. Vincent that I couldn't go to Peter Pan to play with them, and they couldn't come to the main campus to play with me. I liked the attention I got from the older girls. Several of the white girls started calling me their little sister. They went out of their way to make sure I was occupied during play time, but it wasn't the same. We didn't have anything in common. After a while, their conversations usually turned to boys or to something that happened in one of their classes, or to the dance or the upcoming football game. Needless to say, an interest in boys was the furthest thing from my mind. And obviously, I couldn't go to any dances or ball games.

I wanted to play with my new friends. I wanted to make mud pies, like Buster and I did back home. I wanted to play and run and jump with somebody my own age, somebody who wouldn't let me win. I wanted to play with doll babies and shoot marbles, climb trees, and play in the sandbox. I wanted to do all the things that six-year-olds do, things that couldn't happen on the main campus. I wasn't sure if I wanted to live in Peter Pan, but I sure wanted to visit.

# Chapter 5

❧

I guess I wasn't the only one thinking about that. One day, early in October, Mrs. Vincent called me into her office. She said, "They've decided to integrate Peter Pan."

"What is inagrate?" I asked.

"*In-te-grate*. Mixing, colored and white living together," she replied. "Peter Pan is all white but that's about to change. Some people believe you should be with children your own age. You will be moving to Peter Pan tomorrow."

"Is Buster going too?"

"No. Just you."

"How come? Don't he need to be with children his age? And what about James and Jerry and Paul?"

She didn't correct my grammar. "They didn't want to separate the Whitaker boys, so it was between you and Walter, and they decided to send you. Nobody knows how this is going to work out. But if all goes well, your brother and the Whitaker boys will go down later, probably in a few months."

"If I don't like it, can I come back?"

"Whether you like it or not isn't important. They have

43

decided to integrate Peter Pan, and they will decide if it works. Not you. Not me."

I was curious about who "they" were and why "they" hadn't talked to me about moving. I had a feeling that Mrs. Vincent wasn't part of "they." I don't think she liked the idea very much.

I wasn't quite sure how to feel. In a way, I was excited. I'd get to play with my school friends every day. But I wouldn't be with my sisters. *Who's going to take care of me? Who's going to find out whatever I needed to know? Is Betty going to come to Peter Pan everyday and comb my hair? Is she coming down on Saturdays to wash it and straighten it?*

And I wondered about Buster. His classroom was right next to mine, but I hardly ever saw him at school. I saw him in the dining room three times a day, but I couldn't talk to him. Now, I wouldn't even get to see him in the dining room. The only time we played together was when Daddy or Miss Jenkins came for their monthly visits. And even then, we could spend only two hours together. I wasn't sure I would like this.

Betty and Dean were furious when I told them. They went marching into Mrs. Vincent's office. "Why is my sister going to Peter Pan?" Betty demanded. Before Mrs. Vincent could answer, Dean shouted, "Ya'll told Daddy we would be together."

"Now just a minute," she replied. "You don't come into this office demanding to know anything. Don't you take that tone with me."

Betty replied, "But why is she moving? She is suppose to be with us."

Mrs. Vincent told them to sit down. She explained the situation to them. On her way out of the door, Dean said, "You just wait. I'm going to tell my daddy." She ran to our room. Betty stayed with Mrs. Vincent for a few more minutes. I don't know what Mrs. Vincent told her, but when she came into the room, she wasn't mad anymore; she was just sad. After dinner that night, they helped me pack my things. The other girls came to our room. Several of them were mad too. Nobody wanted me to leave. I was so confused. If nobody liked this idea of integration, then why was I going there to integrate?

The next day, Mrs. Vincent put all of my things into her car and drove me to Peter Pan. It was different from the main campus. The buildings formed a horseshoe. There were seven, one-story, red-brick cottages: Pans 1, 2 and 3 for boys, and 5, 6, and 7 for girls. The dining room and the dean's office were in the center. All of the cottages were connected, so we could move from one cottage to another, or to the dining room without going outside.

I was sent to Pan 6, the middle cottage for girls. The inside was very different from Taft. The living room was much larger and had a fireplace. There was a piano too, just like in Taft B. I would soon learn that all of the cottages had pianos. Instead of bedrooms, there was a large dormitory with twenty kid-sized beds lined up against the walls. There were no dressers, just lockers in the locker room. The top half of the lockers had doors and shelves on which we stored our clothes. The bottom half had hooks where we hung our towels and our pajamas. There were three small sinks and three toilets with no doors. The three shower stalls and the bathtub had no curtains. The playroom was just a bit larger than the living room. Along three walls were cubbies, wooden boxes built into the walls, where we stored our toys. The free wall had hooks on it where coats were hung and red, rubber galoshes were lined up.

When I arrived, the children were outside playing. Mrs. Vincent told me to be good. I said I would. Her expressions didn't change, but there was something in her eyes that made me feel sad. She hugged me then stiffened her back, held her head high, and walked out of the cottage.

Miss Allen was the supervisor of Pan 6. She was a little woman, about five feet tall, and thin. She looked a little like my friend, Emma, but not quite as dark. She had black hair, and dark brown eyes like Emma. She smiled and took me to the locker room. We were to inventory my belongings. I knew about inventory. We did that when we went to Taft. I was surprised when I walked in and saw the other five supervisors and the dean waiting for me.

Miss Allen told me to strip and try on all of my clothes so she could determine what I would keep and what else I might need. I took off everything except my undershirt and panties. Miss Miller, the dean, yelled at me.

"I heard you were suppose to be so smart. Don't you know what strip means? It means everything off. Take off that undershirt and those panties."

I was stunned. Joan Jenkins was the only person outside of my family who had seen me completely naked. I said, "Mama said you don't 'posed to let other people see you nekkid. She said that's private."

"Suppose, not 'posed," she replied. "Besides, your mother is dead, isn't she? And I am in charge of Peter Pan. Do what you're told and keep your mouth shut. Now take off those underwear."

I took them off and tried to cover myself with my hands. "Stand up straight, put your hands down, and stop being so silly. Turn around so we can get an idea of what size you are."

Well, if that was all they wanted, I could have told them that. "I wear size four in tops and size six in bottoms 'cause my legs is long," I said, thinking that would be the end of the ordeal.

"*Are* long. My legs *are* long," she shouted back. "Turn around."

I felt awful. I turned slowly as they all whispered and mumbled to each other. I couldn't make out what they were saying. I wanted to know, but I was afraid to ask. I knew if I did, Miss Miller would start yelling again. And she scared me. She was so big—not really very tall—just big. She had thick, muscular legs and the biggest behind I had ever seen. Her long, gray hair was pulled back real tight in a bun. She had dark, beady, deep-set eyes peeking from behind her silver cat-eyes, and pasty-white skin. She had a big hooked nose and no top lip, just an opening where her mouth was. I figured she must be pretty strong and I didn't want her to hit me, so I didn't say a word. I just stood there, feeling very much like a side-show freak, and did what I was told.

I couldn't understand why I had to be naked in front of all those women. Mrs. Vincent hadn't made us do that. She just came to our room and marked our clothes with our initials as we took them out of the boxes. If something looked like it didn't fit, she sent us to the bathroom to try it on. Modesty, that was her thing. She wouldn't even let us go into the living room in our pajamas, unless we had on a housecoat. No, I didn't like this, not one little bit.

I tried on everything, panties, undershirts, pants, dresses, even socks. The whole scene lasted about 30 minutes. When we finished, Miss Allen showed me my locker and the others left the cottage, whispering and smiling—not happy smiles, but sly, evil smiles. Miss Allen called two girls to be my escorts for a few days so I could learn how things were done in Peter Pan. Jenny Baker was one of them. I vaguely remembered seeing her before. She was in Miss Hughes' second grade class. Lauren was my other escort. Jenny grabbed my hand and said, "Come on, let's go outside."

As we bounded down the steps, Lauren took my other hand. They dragged me around the playground, running first to this group of girls, then to another. They were so excited and repeated the same thing to each group we approached. "We got a newkie in our cottage, and she's colored." They sounded so proud. But I wasn't sure what it was that they were more proud of: the fact that they had a newkie, which was a big deal, or the fact that I was colored which was a much bigger deal.

There must have been close to fifty girls in Peter Pan, and that didn't include the eighteen girls in Taylor B. Taylor was the Junior Campus, that housed the eleven and twelve-year olds. And though they lived right across the lane, we couldn't play with them. They had their own playground.

As we neared the slide, I realized that this was it, the place I saw from the hospital. *So this is Peter Pan.* The playground had another side that I couldn't see from the hospital. There was a merry-go-round, a sandbox, another small slide, and another set of monkey bars. And there was a wading pool.

The building just beyond the pool was different from the other cottages. It was a two story building, but a lot bigger than the cottages. "What's that?" I asked.

"That's the dining room," replied Lauren.

I ran to the end of the building. "Let's go over there."

"Come back!" screamed Jenny. "That's the boys' side. You can't go over there."

"Why not?" I asked.

"Cause you can't," she replied. She pointed to the ground. "Do you see this invisible line?" I nodded. "Well," she continued, "that's the boundary line, and we can't cross it or we'll get in trouble. Come on, let's play."

I liked Jenny. She was a cute little bow-legged girl, and so pigeon-toed I don't know how she was able to walk without falling down. Almost every girl in my class was in Pan 6, along with half of the second grade girls. This didn't seem so bad after all.

I tested every piece of equipment on the playground. I liked this better than the main campus. The swings and slide up there were too high for me. And the teeter-totters up there weren't much fun either. I was always stuck in the up position. These were shorter and not quite as wide, and the kids were my size so it was more balanced. We wore ourselves out and we had a ball!

Miss Allen called for us to get ready for dinner. After we washed and changed clothes, we lined up according to height, with the shortest in front. Miss Allen paired me with Emma. We were second from the back.

We marched to the dining room in columns of two, holding our partners' hands. Our other hands were balled into fists, with the index fingers extended and pressed against our lips to remind us not to talk as we walked. We sat in cottage groups, just like on the main campus. And just like on the main campus, the girls sat on one side, and the boys sat on the other. The tables and chairs were small, kid sized. I really liked that. On the main campus, I had a hard time reaching the table.

In the back of the dining room in the center was an adult-sized table with a single chair. The table was draped with a white, linen tablecloth, and was set with china, crystal, and a bud vase that held silk flowers. That's where Miss Miller sat. After we said grace and ate for a few minutes, Miss Miller rang a little brass bell. A hush fell over the dining room. She was about to make one of her announcements, which meant that we had to put down our forks and stop eating.

She asked me to stand. "As you can see," she began, "we have a new girl in Peter Pan. She's colored."

I thought, *Gee whiz. Here we go again.* Only she didn't sound excited or proud the way Lauren and Jenny did.

She continued. "Now that's not her fault." She is a child of God, just like the rest of us. I like to think of us as flowers in God's garden. And in a garden, there are many flowers—roses, daffodils, carnations and so forth. They all look different and smell different, but they all can be beautiful. I don't want to hear words like nigger, pickaninny, or jungle bunny. We don't use words like that here at OSSO. I hope we don't have any problems. We are all God's children and

God loves us all the same. We're all brothers and sisters in the Lord. That's all." She sat back down and we continued to eat.

*Not my fault!* I wondered what that meant. I thought fault meant somebody had done something wrong. *Was there something wrong with being colored? If there was and it wasn't my fault, whose fault was it?* I could feel the blood rushing to my face. I was so mad. I hadn't been in Peter Pan a full day and this woman had embarrassed me twice. All I could think was, *Golly, these people sure are weird. Why do they always do stuff to make people feel bad?* I just knew everybody was staring at me. I wished she hadn't said anything at all.

$\diamond$

After dinner, we marched back to the cottage, holding hands and being quiet. We undressed and lined up in two columns to take showers, two to each stall, and get dressed for bed. Our dining room partner was also our shower buddy. Miss Allen pulled me from the line. "How would you like to take a bath in the tub instead of a shower?"

Emma immediately asked, "Mommy Allen, since we're shower buddies, can we be bath buddies too?"

"No, you will shower alone tonight."

The other girls had been asking to use the tub for a long time. The tub was raised about three feet from the floor. There were four built-in steps by which to access it. They had always been told that it was too dangerous, that they were too small to use the tub. I suppose they wondered the same thing I did. *Since we're the same age and size, why is it dangerous for them, but not for me?*

After I finished my bath, I had to scrub the tub with Ajax. We put on our pajamas and slippers and went to the living room for our nightly devotions. I asked Emma why she had called her Mommy. "Is she your mother?"

Everybody laughed. "No," replied Emma, "we all have to

call her Mommy. You have to call her Mommy too."

I was more than a little baffled. "But she's not my mother. My mother is dead."

Several girls, including Emma responded, "So is mine."

Then Jenny chimed in, "It don't matter. We all have to call her Mommy anyway. Everybody in Peter Pan calls their supervisor Mommy." I just assumed that this was another one of those things I had to learn about how things are done at the OSSO.

Miss Allen finally came into the living room and sat in her chair. We sat cross-legged on the floor in a semi-circle facing her. She read from the Bible and told us a Bible story. Then she asked me if I knew The Lord's Prayer. I said I did. We all got on our knees, folded our hands and she asked me to recite it. With bowed head and closed eyes, I began.

"Now I lay me, down to sleep. I pray the Lord my soul to keep. If I should die before I wake, I pray the Lord my soul to take. God bless Daddy, and Bill, Bob, Ed, Buster, Lewis, Ben, Daved, Betty, Dean, Corine, and Miss Jenkins. And God bless Mama too. Jesus wept. Amen."

I knew "Jesus wept" wasn't part of the prayer. But Dean said it all the time, so I thought I'd just add it to my prayer anyway. I was so proud of myself. I opened my eyes and raised my head. Miss Allen was glaring at me. Half of the girls were looking at me with their mouths wide open. The other half, frozen in fear, just looked at Miss Allen. I didn't understand why they were so frightened and why she was so mad.

She got up, grabbed me by the arm and said, "That is not The Lord's Prayer. Why would you sit there and lie like that? Girls, we are going to have to pray for this heathen. The Bible says Thou shalt not lie. You heard her, didn't you? Didn't she say she knew The Lord's Prayer?"

They all nodded and said, "Yes, Mommy Allen."

"And was that The Lord's Prayer?"

They all shook their heads and replied, "No, Mommy Allen."

She stretched her arms out and said, "Come on girls, the circle." They formed a circle around me as she pushed me toward the center. They held hands and she prayed for my soul. *What did I do? Why did she call me a heathen?* I didn't even know what a heathen was, but I could tell by the way she said it and by the look on her face that it was something bad.

She prayed that the Lord would put a truthful tongue in my head and asked Him to cast Satan out of my heart so Jesus could come in. After the prayer, they stood around me and sang. "Get thee behind me, Satan. Get thee away. I want to be a Christian soldier and I want to learn to pray. Get thee behind me, Satan. Get thee away. I want to be a Christian soldier and love Jesus everyday."

When they finished the song, she asked Jenny to recite The Lord's Prayer for the "heathen." *There's that word again. What does it mean?*

As Jenny said the words, I thought, *I know this! I just didn't know it was called The Lord's Prayer. It doesn't say Lord or pray one time.* At home, we called that The Our Father. I tried to tell her that after Jenny finished, but she told me to be quiet.

"There are a few things you need to learn and learn quickly, young lady. I don't care what you did at home or what you did on the main campus. You are in Peter Pan now, and you will learn to do things the Peter Pan way. And another thing, here in Peter Pan, you will call me Mommy. Is that clear?"

I wanted to ask her why, but instead, I simply said, "Yes."

"Yes what?" she fired back.

"Yes ma'm."

Lauren leaned over and whispered, "Mommy Allen. Yes, Mommy Allen."

I caved in. "Yes, Mommy Allen."

"That's more like it. Now, everybody off to the toilet, then to bed."

I got up and headed toward the door. Emma grabbed my wrist and pulled me in line behind her. One at a time, they stepped up to Miss Allen's chair, hugged her, kissed her on the cheek and said, "Good night, Mommy Allen."

I didn't want to call this woman Mommy. My mother was dead. I hadn't even called her Mommy; I called her Mama. I resented calling anyone else any form of the word. I had lived in Mrs. Jenkins' house for six months and not once did I call her anything other than Miss Jenkins. Now here I was, facing this angel-faced, devil-hearted white woman, who in no shape, form, or fashion was anything remotely close to my mother. I didn't want to hug this woman. I didn't want to kiss her. I didn't want to wish her a good night. And I certainly didn't want to call her Mommy.

What I wanted to do was ask her why she was so mean and if everybody in Peter Pan was as mean as she was. I wanted to ask her what a heathen was. "Get thee behind me, Satan." That's what they had sung. *Was heathen and Satan the same thing?* But like the others in line before me, I hugged her, kissed her cheek, and said, "Good night, Mommy Allen."

As we headed down the hall, the pungent smell of ammonia grew stronger and stronger. By the time we reached the locker room, we could hardly breathe. Miss Allen came into the locker room putting on a pair of yellow rubber gloves. She reached into the tub and pulled out the stopper. She looked at us and said, "I had to get rid of that dirt and kill those germs somehow." She walked out.

The girls turned and looked at me as if I were some type of filthy, deadly contagion. *Germs? She didn't scrub the showers with ammonia. We had been outside together. I played on the same swing set and the same merry-go-round everybody else played on. I got into the same sandbox that everybody else got in. How come the dirt on me was different from the dirt on them? How come they didn't have germs that needed to be drowned in ammonia?*

I used the toilet, washed my hands and went to the dormitory. I had already been told that we didn't use pillows in Peter Pan, and that we had to sleep on our stomachs. I had been warned to "try not to turn over on your back in your sleep or you'll get in trouble." I thought, *Well, how can I do that? If I'm sleep, how can I tell myself not to turn over?*

I crawled into bed and lay on my stomach. I pulled the covers over my head. I didn't want anybody to hear me cry. I prayed that there really was a heaven and that Mama was up there so she could look down and see what was going on. I figured that maybe God was too busy, having to watch everybody in the whole world. Mama just had us and Daddy to watch. Maybe she could tell God what was happening to me and God would let Daddy come and get me.

I don't think I had ever felt so lonely. I wanted my sisters and brothers and my daddy. And I wanted my mama. I wanted her to give me a blue popsicle and tell me that everything would be all right.

I didn't deliberately lie about the prayer. Mama called things like that a mistake. *Maybe, in Peter Pan, we aren't allowed to make mistakes.* I was confused. *Who told Daddy this was a nice place and that we'd all be together? Who told him we would like this place?* I was scared. *What will Miss Allen do to me if I turn over on my back while I'm sleep?*

This place was big and bright and had a lot of toys and playground equipment. It had a nice hospital and a good school with a gym and swimming pool. We had plenty of food to eat and clothes and shoes to wear. We had our own towels and washcloths, and we had our own beds and blankets and bedspreads. We had just about everything any child could need or want. But I wasn't any child. What I wanted, they couldn't, or wouldn't give me.

I wanted to go home. I didn't care that our house was drafty and that we had to use the toilet outside. I didn't care that I had to sleep in a bed with my sisters in the same room as my brothers. I didn't care that Mama had to heat water on the stove so we could take a bath in a tin tub in the middle of the kitchen and share towels and wash cloths. I just wanted to go home.

# Chapter 6

ꝸ

Sundays were special. We got to sleep late, well, twenty minutes later than normal. Usually, we were served something a little different with breakfast, a donut or chocolate milk. Sometimes, we'd have ham or sausage instead of bacon, or we'd have French toast or pancakes.

The same was true in Peter Pan. After breakfast, we went back to the cottage to get ready for church. I hadn't seen a chapel in Peter Pan and I knew they didn't come to the chapel on the main campus. Maybe there was another part of Peter Pan that I didn't know about.

We were dressed and sitting in our lockers waiting for Miss Allen when Miss Miller came in. She pointed at me and said, "Come with me."

My heart started racing and I felt queasy. I stood. My legs felt like rubber. I didn't think they'd support my weight. I wondered, *Now what did I do!* I just knew I was in trouble. So did everybody else. As I passed them, several of the girls looked at the floor. Lauren, Jenny, and Emma looked as if they were about to cry. I followed Miss Miller outside to her car. We got in and just sat for a minute, both of us staring straight ahead. Finally she spoke. She told me that I couldn't go to church with my cottage. She said, "They go to a white church in town. You will be going to a colored church."

I looked at her and said, "On the main campus, everybody goes to chapel together." As soon as I'd said it, I regretted it. I knew I was in trouble now. I held my breath and looked straight ahead. I didn't want to see the smack in the mouth that I was sure was coming.

She said, "I know. But the chapel belongs to the Home. We can do things the way we want when we own the buildings. But, honey, the Home doesn't own the churches in town. We don't know what would happen if we took a colored child to a white church." She paused. "You wouldn't want the other children to be put out of their church because of you, would you? Besides, you people have your own way of worshipping, which is different from ours. You'll like it there, honey. You'll be with your own people. Won't that be fun?"

I didn't know if it would be fun or not, and I really didn't care. She hadn't hit me. And she called me honey. Twice. I simply said, "Yes, Mommy Miller."

She started the car. As she drove, I thought about her dining room announcement on my first day in Peter Pan. "We are all God's children and God loves us all the same. We're all brothers and sisters in the Lord." That's what she said. Now, all of a sudden, I had my own people. I didn't get it. I could live with white people. I could go to school with white people. I could eat and sleep and play with white people. I was even forced to call white women Mommy. But I couldn't go to church with white people. I wanted to ask her about that, but I didn't. I just figured that was how things were done in Peter Pan.

◇

When we got to the church, St. John's AME, she went into the minister's office. I stood in the hall, right outside the door. They talked softly for a while, then she got up to leave. The minister shook her hand and said, "We'll take good care of her. She'll be just fine."

Miss Miller told me she'd be back for me after church and that I should wait just inside the door until I saw her car.

The minister was a big man, tall and heavy with a big, low voice that filled the entire room. He put his hand on my shoulder and said, "Don't you worry about a thing, baby. You'll like it here."

I thought, *Yea, I've heard that before.*

He continued, "Would you like to go with Sis. Walker? She's in charge of our Sunday School Programs."

I didn't answer. I just kept staring at that big hand on my shoulder. I thought, *Man, if he slapped somebody with that great big ole hand, he'd probably break their whole face! Hmm, I wonder if he wears gloves. Where in the world does he ever find gloves to fit those great big hands?* No sooner had the thought crossed my mind than the answer came. *He probably wears baseball gloves.*

He sent for Sis. Walker. As soon as I saw her, I thought, *This must be a fat people's church!* The people we passed in the hall were on the hefty side, the minister was big, and so was Sis. Walker. She was built like my mother, but she was taller. Shoot, she was taller than Miss Jenkins. Her upper arms were big and flabby, and I wondered if she had that hanging-down piece of meat over her elbows like Mama did.

She walked over and hugged me. She was soft and warm, just like Mama. "And what's your name, baby?"

"Nancy."

"Nancy what?"

"Gibson."

"And how old are you?"

"Six."

"Do you like Sunday School?"

"I don't know. I never been to Sunday School. I been to

church though. And I been to chapel lots of times too."

"Well, baby, you come on downstairs with Sis. Walker. Sis. Walker think you gonna' like Sunday School."

I walked a few steps behind her as we went downstairs. I looked at her arms. *She's got it—that hanging-down piece of meat over her elbows. Just like Mama.* Somehow, I knew at that very moment that I would like her.

And she was right. I liked Sunday School. They read Bible stories to us and we had arts and crafts. We sang songs; some I knew, others I didn't. After Sunday School, those of us who were staying went upstairs for church. The other children sat with their parents as Sis. Walker took me down to the front pew. She said, "Now baby, Sis. Walker wants you to sit right here, in the front. Reverend is gonna' ask visitors to stand and introduce themselves to the church. You speak up nice and loud so everybody can hear you. Say your whole name, where you live, how old you are and what grade you're in. Sis. Walker sings in the choir, else she'd sit here with you." *Why do you call yourself Sis. Walker? Why don't you say I or me like everybody else?*

The service was wonderful. It wasn't like chapel where Rev. Walters read prayers from a book and preached in a dry, dull monotone, and the choir stood still and sang slow, sad songs. At St. John's, they sang a lot of fast, happy songs and the choir rocked from side to side and clapped and played tambourines. And the congregation jumped up and sang with them or shouted, "Sang choir!" just like they did back home. And when the preacher prayed, he really prayed. He called God all kinds of names I had never heard before. And he prayed for a long time. At first, I thought the prayer was the sermon!

And just like Sis. Walker said, the minister asked the visitors to stand and introduce themselves. Several people stood. St. John's was a big church, way bigger than the chapel, and I was so nervous. *What if I make a mistake? Will*

*they call me a heathen, or make a circle around me and pray
for me if I say the wrong thing? Will they call me Satan and
tell me to get behind them? I don't want to do this.*
I looked up at Sis. Walker, who nodded her head and
smiled. As I waited my turn, I remembered what she said,
"Speak up nice and loud." When it was my turn, I turned to
face the congregation. *Golly! Where did all these people
come from? They weren't here when I came in.*
My mouth was dry, and my stomach was churning. I took
a deep breath, and I shouted as loud as I could, "My name is
Nancy Jean Gibson. I live at the OS&SO Home in Xenia,
Ohio. I am in Pan 6. I am six years old and I am in the first
grade. Thank you."
I turned, sat down, and breathed a big sigh of relief. It was
over. I had done it. Suddenly, everybody was laughing. *I
knew it. I knew I'd say the wrong thing. I just knew they
would laugh at me.* I wanted to cry and run out of the
church. I looked up at Sis. Walker. She smiled as the minister, in that big bass voice said, "That's all right, baby."
After another selection from the choir, the minister began
his sermon. He wasn't like Rev. Walters at all. He moved all
around the pulpit. Sometimes he jumped up and down and
people were talking throughout the church. "Oh, preach
brother." "Tell the truth, now!" And people were shouting
and getting happy.
And at the other end of the pew where I sat, was a balding, chocolate brown, toothless little old man. He just sat
there and rocked back and forth. And every once in a while
he'd throw one hand in the air and say "Well!" And he didn't
just say it; he sort of sang it, dragged it out like the last note
of a song. "Weelll!"
After church, everybody came up and hugged me or
shook my hand. They said they were glad to have me in
church and hoped I'd come back. I didn't understand why
they'd want me to come back when they had laughed. I

asked Sis. Walker why they had done that, why they laughed at me.

She said, "Baby, they weren't laughing at you. They were laughing with you. When Sis. Walker told you to speak up nice and loud so everybody could hear you, Sis. Walker meant everybody in the church, not everybody in town." Then she smiled.

I didn't understand what she meant by laughing *with* me, especially since I wasn't laughing. But I did understand that they weren't making fun of me. And I truly believed that they wanted me to come back.

I had been standing in the doorway for about five minutes when Miss Miller pulled up. I ran to the car. "Oh, Mommy Miller, church was real good. If I say Mommy all the time and clean out the tub real good, and stop being a heathen, can I go back? Please?"

"*May* I. *May* I go back, not can I."

"*May* I go back next Sunday? Oh, please?"

"Well, since you can't go to the church with your cottage, and you certainly can't go to chapel, and you do have to go somewhere. . ." She didn't finish the sentence and she almost smiled. I took that as a yes.

I couldn't wait to get back to the cottage so I could tell the girls about my church. I knew their church wasn't as good as mine. No church, anywhere, could be as good as St. John's. And nobody could possibly be as nice as Sis. Walker. The minister was nice and so was everybody else at the church. But Sis. Walker—well, she was just—special.

◇

St. John's became my church home. Every Sunday, Miss Miller would drop me off and drive across town to the white church. Then she picked me up after services. I loved St. John's. No matter what the homework assignment was, I always did more. I wanted to impress Sis. Walker. I so desperately wanted her to like me. If we were to memorize five books of the Old Testament, I memorized ten. If we were to learn one Bible verse, I learned three—the one before it and the one after it. I would have done anything to get Sis. Walker to like me. I don't know when or how it came to me, but one day I realized that Sis. Walker did like me; not because I could memorize Bible verses or rattle off the books of the Bible. Sis. Walker liked me because I was me. It was just that simple.

I had been in Peter Pan for nearly three months. I was doing well in school and had made a lot of friends. I even thought Mommy Allen was starting to like me. We were lining up for dinner one evening. Nothing out of the ordinary occurred to any of us that day, at least, that I remember.

As usual, the girls entered the dining room first, after which the boys entered, beginning with Pan 3. I don't know why I looked up, but I did. And to my surprise, there was Buster, grinning at me. His table was so close to mine that I could have touched him. He smiled and started to speak. I shook my head. He didn't say anything. The Whitaker boys were there too. Jerry was in Buster's cottage, James was in Pan 2; and Paul was in Pan 1.

We were the last little colored children to live on the main campus. Thereafter, all children under the age of eleven, regardless of race, were sent to Peter Pan. I suppose some would say the experiment was a success.

The following Sunday when Miss Miller came to pick me up, the boys were already in the car. I asked James to sit up front so I could sit in the back with Buster. Other than our occasional visits from Daddy or Miss Jenkins, I rarely saw him. We held hands and whispered, and though nothing was particularly funny, we giggled all the way to church. And I told him about Sis. Walker; how pretty and nice she was, and how soft she was. It was such a wonderful ride.

As soon as we got inside the church, we ran downstairs. I was still holding Buster's hand and practically dragging him down the steps. Sis. Walker was talking with several other women about the Christmas Program. I knew I was suppose to say, "Excuse me" when interrupting grown folks, but I couldn't. I just ran up to her and started talking.

"Sis. Walker. Sis. Walker. Looky. This is Buster, my baby brother. He's in Peter Pan now. And so is Jerry. Jerry Whitaker. He's in Buster's cottage. And James. He's in my class. He's in Pan 2. And this is Paul. He's their big brother. He's in the second grade. He should be in Pan 2, but he's in Pan 1. And they have a big sister, Jackie, but she's too big to be in Peter Pan. She lives on the main campus, in Taft B. That's the colored girls' cottage. I used to be in that cottage before I moved to Peter Pan. Jackie's in my sister's grade. Not my big sister, but my middle sister. Ya'll, this is Sis. Walker. She's in charge of Sunday School. The preacher, he needs her to be in charge because she's smart and she's nice and she knows how to boss people around and not be mean. Oh, and she gives us Sunday School homework too. But it's not real hard. And sometimes we start on our homework in Sunday School and if you don't know it, Sis. Walker will help you. Oh, yea, and she's in charge of the Christmas program too. Everybody is in it. Some people get to sing and some people get to talk. I get to talk 'cause Sis. Walker asked me to. She's my friend. She can be your friend too, if you want." I was so excited. I thought that if I didn't say everything at one time, I would forget some very important information.

Sis. Walker put her arm around me and pulled me close to her side. She started rubbing my back, I guess to calm me down. She said a few words to the boys, and told us to take our seats. I introduced them to some of the other children. We spent the whole time rehearsing the Christmas Program. Since all the speaking parts had already been assigned, the boys were to sing with the choir. I was to recite Luke 2:8-20 while the other children acted it out. We had two full weeks before the program, but I had memorized it already.

After Sunday School, we went upstairs for church. The boys had to stand as I had a few months earlier, and introduce themselves to the congregation. They were about as nervous as I had been. The Whitaker boys went first. Buster whispered to me that he didn't want to do it. I told him not to worry, I'd handle it. When it was his turn, I held his hand and stood with him. We faced the congregation and I said, "Good morning, church. This is my baby brother, Buster. Well, his real name is Walter Steve Gibson, but we call him Buster. My daddy started calling him that 'cause he liked Buster Keaton. He's four years old and he's in the kindergarten. He lives at the OS&SO Home too. He's in Pan 3. He was in Adams B, but he just moved to Peter Pan 'cause he's too little to be on the main campus. He's kinda scared to talk in front of ya'll. I used to be scared, but I'm not anymore. Buster probably won't be scare after while either. Besides, he doesn't talk real good yet, 'cause he has a real bad lisp. That's another reason I have to talk for him. But Daddy said it will probably go away when he gets big. Thank you." We sat down. Man, was I important, showing the boys the ropes, speaking up for Buster. I was big time stuff.

After church, the boys were hugged and greeted and made to feel like part of one big happy family. They liked St. John's too.

Finally, the Sunday before Christmas arrived—the day of the program. Some children read poems, the choir sang a medley, there were a couple of solos. Then it was my turn. I walked to the lectern, stood on the box and adjusted the microphone. I looked at Sis. Walker, sitting in the second pew, beaming with pride. I did exactly what she told me to do. I said it slowly, clearly, and looked around at everybody in the church. "And there were in the same country shepherds abiding in the fields, keeping watch over their flocks by night."

I didn't miss a beat. I used the right intonations and expressions. I understood the story, but I really didn't understand the language. I wish I could have just said it in regular English. Poor Buster didn't know what I was talking about. See, I would have just said, "One night, a bunch of shepherds were sitting on a hill watching their lambs, and out of nowhere, this angel came down from heaven and scared the daylights out of them. But the angel told them, 'Don't be scared, ya'll. I got some good news for you." And did people really say things like "a multitude of the heavenly host" or did they just say, "Then a whole lot of angels came down and joined the first angel." But that's the way it was written, and I didn't think I should rewrite the Bible. But I sure wanted to.

And then finally, I was at the last verse. "And the shepherds returned glorifying and praising God for all the things they had heard and seen as it was told unto them." The choir stood and all the readers and actors joined them for the finale—*Joy To The World*.

When we were finished, everybody in the church stood and started clapping. I felt like I was on top of the world. Everybody was shouting, "Amen" or "Praise God" except Sis. Walker. She stood with one hand clasped tightly to her bosom and the other raised slightly in the air. She looked heavenward and mouthed, "Thank you Jesus" as tears trickled slowly down her face. And to her right, further down the pew, was that balding, chocolate brown, toothless little old man, rocking back and forth, smiling. He slowly rose and clapped two or three times. And as he sat, he threw one hand in the air and sang his one word, one note song, "Weelll!"

I knew they were clapping for all of us. But for a moment, I felt as if they were clapping only for me. All that love and pride was for me and me alone. And I soaked it up like a sponge.

Miss Miller was almost right when she said, "You'll like

it there, honey." I didn't just like it at St. John's. I loved it. And I knew, without an iota of doubt, that the people at St. John's loved me.

◇

We were all excited about Christmas. The mantle in the living room was decorated with angel hair and multicolored glass bulbs. It was pretty, but I didn't like the angel hair; it made me itch. Miss Allen had strung popcorn and cranberries that we wrapped around the nearly six-foot tree. We wrapped the tree with gold garland and hung icicles and glass bulbs. The tree looked wonderful. Miss Allen cut three large circles from white poster board and we glued cotton balls on them. She strung the circles together to make a snowman, and hung it on the wall in the hall. She strung cotton balls and paper snowflakes from white thread and taped them to the ceiling. The cottage looked so nice.

On Christmas morning, we awoke to the sounds of a choir singing the Home Christmas Carol. It was tradition. Every year, ex-pupils returned to sing with the senior choir on Christmas morning. They serenaded the entire campus. In Peter Pan, they started in Pan 7, and walked through all of the cottages carrying candles and singing. It was the most wonderful surprise. We piled into the doorway to watch them as they passed, followed by Santa Claus in his bright red suit, with a long string of bells.

Orphans were allowed to go home on Christmas day, and return to campus on the 31st. Most of us were going home after lunch. I don't know why, but we were just going to spend the day and come back that night. I wanted to stay the whole week, but I was glad just to spend Christmas in my house with my daddy. Some of my cottage mates weren't going home at all.

I don't remember how we got to Dayton that day or how we got back to the Home. I was glad to see that our house looked the same. Daddy had bought a big tree, as he had always done. He had strung the same lights and hung the same bulbs. And there was no angel hair.

There were presents everywhere. I got the usual, clothes and toys, most of which I don't remember. But the one thing I do remember was the sponge doll. She was colored with a hard plastic face and sewn-in hair. Her dress, arms, and legs were made of alternating layers of pink and blue sponge. She had on black shoes, just like the patent leather ones Miss Jenkins bought for my birthday. Daddy said he bought her because she looked just like me. She was caramel colored. Her skin had a little more red than mine, and she had a fat, round face, thick short hair, and big eyes. Oh, how I loved my doll baby. She didn't do anything like Betsy Wetsy or Tiny Tears, but I loved her.

We ate and played and had a good time. Miss Jenkins came over with more gifts. Some of the neighbors came over too. They commented on how well we looked and wanted to know how things were going. I didn't want to talk about the Home or much of anything else for that matter. I just wanted to play with my doll.

The visit was short. We packed our gifts, kissed Daddy good-bye and headed back to the Home. Buster and I played all the way back. He was the daddy, I was the mama, and my doll baby was our child. We were good parents. We didn't yell at our child or hit her or call her names like they did at the Home.

Miss Allen met me at the door. She directed me to the playroom and told me to put my toys in my cubbie. "When you're finished, if you have any new clothes, bring them to my office so we can try them on and mark them," she said.

I went to the playroom and sat on the floor and talked to my doll. I guess I took too long, because she came to get me. When she saw my doll, she was furious. "What in the name of Pete is that?"

She scared the daylights out of me. "It's my doll baby. My

daddy gave her to me. Do you think she looks like me? Daddy said she does."

She snatched the doll from my hands and threw it against the brick wall on the far end of the room and started yelling. "I don't want that evil, ugly thing in this cottage. It bears the mark of Cain, and I won't have it in my cottage."

I sat there on the floor, staring at her. I had never seen her so mad.

"Get that filthy thing out of my cottage."

"But my daddy gave her to me. She's my Christmas present."

"I don't care where you got it. I want it out of here." She was screaming and her face was red. The veins in her neck and forehead were bulging.

"But what am I suppose to do with her?"

"Take it outside and put it in the trash."

"But Daddy gave her to me." By this time, I was crying.

She grabbed my arm and snatched me up from the floor. "You will do what you're told, young lady. Get that devil doll out of my cottage. Now!"

I walked slowly across the room and picked up my doll. She had a gaping hole in her face. I turned and looked at Miss Allen. *You broke my doll. Why did you break my doll?* She stood there, with her hands on her hips, glaring at me. She pointed to the back door. I walked out the door and down the steps to the garbage can. I took the lid off and stared into the empty can, then dropped my doll, replaced the lid and walked back up the steps. The sound of my doll hitting the bottom of that empty can echoed in my mind for days.

During devotions that night, Miss Allen prayed for me. I didn't close my eyes. I just stared at her. My mind was racing from one thought to the next. *If my doll baby is evil, and the doll looks like me, am I evil?* "Devil doll," that's what she called it. *Is the devil colored?*

*Is that why she called me a heathen?* Maybe I was evil. I sure had evil thoughts about her. We didn't sleep on pillows but she did. *Maybe I could sneak in her room and smother her with her pillow.* She was small and I was tall for six and pretty strong. *Maybe I could pick her up and throw her against the wall like she did my doll baby. Or maybe I could just take her outside and throw her in the garbage can.* I had never hated anyone, but at that moment I hated her. With every fiber of my being, I hated that woman.

After prayer, we sang songs and lined up for our nightly ritual of kissing her goodnight. I stood in line staring at her neck and wondered, *How long do you have to choke someone before they die?* When I reached the front of the line, I walked over to her, hugged her, kissed her cheek and said, "Good night, Mommy Allen," and then, I went to bed.

I tossed and turned all night long. *Should I tell Betty about the doll? Should I tell Daddy? Why are these people so mean? How can she call herself a Christian and act this way? If this is how Christians act, I don't ever want to be one. Not ever.*

# Chapter 7

࿓

All of the adults who worked in Peter Pan were white, except the three cooks and Miss Mildred. We had chores around the cottage, but Miss Mildred did the major cleaning. She stripped and waxed the floors, ran the buffer and washed the windows and walls.

When I moved to Peter Pan, she got another assignment, washing and pressing my hair on Saturday mornings, an assignment she hated. She complained that before I came to Peter Pan, Saturdays and Sundays were her days off. "If your sister is big enough to do her own hair, she ought to be big enough to do yours."

Sometimes, if she had plans, she wouldn't wait for my hair to dry. She would press it while it was still wet. If I flinched, she'd whack me on the shoulder with a comb, a brush, or whatever was handy. Occasionally, though not often, she was nice to me. On those rare occasions when she was in a good mood, she'd have me sit by the heat register so my hair would dry completely before she pressed it and we'd eat M&Ms and talk. A few times, we even played Bee Bee Bumblebee or sang.

71

We had a mild winter and a short one, or so it seemed. By mid-March, we were wearing our spring jackets. Miss Allen took us on a field trip to the farm. We could see some of the animals nearly everyday when we played outside, but we couldn't go near the fence that surrounded the pasture. We were pretty excited about going, until we actually got there. From a distance, we liked the cows. But up close, they were nasty. They smelled horrible. Their noses ran all the time. They kept swatting us with their tails. The farmers gave us hay and alfalfa to feed them. We each had to feed one, whether we wanted to or not. They licked our hands and their tongues felt like wet sandpaper. One of the farmers was milking and asked if we wanted to try it. Peggy said she did. I was afraid that we would all have to take a turn, but fortunately, we didn't.

From there we went to see the pigs. They were worse than the cows. Some were wallowing in the mud, and every time they moved they made a gurgling, sucking sound. Others came up to the edge of the pen and sniffed or grunted at us. I didn't like the pigs either. The chickens weren't too bad, though. They pretty much ignored us and strutted around the barnyard as if we were not important.

When we came back through the barn, the son of one of the farmers was sitting on a bench, playing with what appeared to be a rock.

"What is that?" Emma wanted to know.

"My pet turtle," he replied.

"It looks like a rock to me," she answered.

"That's 'cause the turtle is inside. This is his shell."

"Well, when is he gonna' come out?" she asked.

"I don't know," he said. "Sometimes, when he gets scared, he goes inside his shell for protection. He'll come out if he thinks it's safe."

We didn't know whether to believe him or not. It certainly didn't look like an animal to me. It just looked like a rock with six holes in it. This boy was about twelve or thirteen years old and he wasn't an Orphan, so we thought he was probably just teasing us. But, just in case, we asked Mrs. Mart about it when we went back to school. She told us that turtles do have hard shells and that when they are frightened, they hide inside their shells. A few days later, she brought some turtles to class for us to see. Finally, an animal I liked.

◇

I decided, one day, that I would become a turtle. It was still spring, near the end of the school year. I was seven and Buster was now five. We had gone to the dining room for dinner. As usual, as soon as I reached my chair, I looked for Buster. When he came into the room, I knew something was wrong with him. He had been crying. His supervisor, Miss Reutger, was the biggest supervisor in Peter Pan. She was nearly six feet tall and weighed at least two hundred pounds. She had big ears and a big nose. Her gray hair was short and she wore big, round, tortoise shell glasses. I thought, *If that big cow hit him, I'm gonna' fix her.*

Miss Reutger was mean. She never smiled, not at cartoons or movies, not at jokes, not even at Jay Smith. Jay was a newkie in her cottage and was a cute little fat, red-haired, freckle-faced boy. He had green eyes and a grin that would brighten a dungeon. Everybody smiled at Jay, everybody except Miss Reutger.

We had already said grace, but Buster wasn't eating. He kept pushing his food around his plate. Miss Reutger yelled at him. "Walter Gibson, stop playing with your food and eat."

"But Mommy Reutger, my thomach hurth."

"There is nothing wrong with you." She got up and went to his table. "You eat this food. Now. Every bit of it, and I mean it." She stood beside him and watched to make sure he ate.

After he took a couple of bites, she went back to her table and sat down. He turned to her and said, "Mommy Reutger, I feel thick." Before he could say anything else, he vomited.

Most of it got on the floor, but some got on his plate and his clothes. She got up from her table, walked over to him, and slapped him. I turned, just to be sure that what I thought was going on really was happening. She yelled at him again.

"You go get a bucket and a rag and clean this mess up, you little pig."

He looked at me with tears rolling down his face, then he looked at her and said, "But my thomach hurth."

My face was stinging and my ears were ringing as I fought to keep from falling out of my chair. Miss Allen had hit me. "Stop rubber-necking. You turn around and eat your dinner."

"But he's sick and she hit him," I protested.

"Well," she said. "Since you want to see it so bad, you clean it up."

I got up and went into the sink room. Buster was crying, trying to reach the faucets on the over-sized sink. "I'll get it Buster."

"I'm thick. My thomach hurth real bad. I want Daddy to come get me."

I started crying too. "Don't worry Buster. I'll tell Betty and she'll tell Daddy." I got some paper towels down from the shelf and cleaned his face and shirt as best I could. I filled the bucket with water and got a rag from the barrel. "Wait here 'til I come back."

I went out and cleaned up the table, his chair, and the floor. When I went to empty the bucket, Buster was curled up on the floor, holding his stomach, moaning and crying. I rinsed out the rag and hung it on the edge of the sink to dry. I dumped the bucket in the toilet and sat on the floor beside him.

"Come on, Buster. You got to get up."

"I can't. My thomach hurth."

"You got to." I wiped his face, then mine and helped him to his feet.

"Mommy Reutger ith gonna' hit me again."

"No she won't. I promise. Now come on. We gotta' go."
We went back into the dining room, he to his table; me to mine. No sooner had he sat down than Miss Reutger came out of the kitchen with another plate of food. She put the plate in front of him. "You are going to eat every bit of this food. And if you throw up in it again, I'll make you eat that too." She traded seats with one of the boys at the table. She sat right beside him and forced him to eat.

"I'm gonna' be thick. I got to throw up."
She banged her fist on the table. "You better not!"
He started heaving and struggled to keep his mouth closed. As he fought to keep his lips together, vomit ran from his nose onto his plate. His eyes were wide with fear. And when he couldn't hold it any longer, he turned his head, opened his mouth, and it came gushing out. She leaned back in the chair to keep it from splashing on her.

I wanted to go to him, to help him. I wished I had a lump of starch or some baking soda. That's what Mama always gave us at home when we were sick. Not knowing what else to do, I just sat there, and watched.

She slapped him and yelled, "Are you quite finished?" He nodded. She said, "Answer me. I can't hear your brains rattle."

"Yeth" he whispered.

"Yes what?" she demanded.

"Yeth, Mommy Reutger."

She picked up the spoon, scraped it across his plate, and proceeded to feed him the food covered with vomit. I couldn't believe it. I jumped up out of my chair. So did Miss Allen. She grabbed my arm, spun me around, and back-handed me so hard I almost fell over my chair. She grabbed me and shook me.

Before she could say anything, I yelled, "But she's feeding him vomit!" I struggled to fight back the tears. Miss Allen pushed me toward the wall.

"You stand there and don't you move until I tell you to.

Get that foot up."

I was so mad. I wanted to hit her. I wanted to hit Miss. Reutger. I wanted to scream. I wanted to grab Buster and run—to Betty, to Ben, to Daddy—it didn't matter. I just wanted to get us out of there, but I couldn't. And I wanted to cry, but I couldn't do that either. I just stood there, on one foot, in a six-inch square tile and stared at the wall, determined not to let a single tear trickle from my eyes.

And I felt guilty for betraying Buster. I promised him that she wouldn't hit him again. I just couldn't imagine that anyone would hit a child because he was sick. But she did.

*What kind of people are you? How could you do that? And where are you, Mr. God? Why won't you do something? The Bible says, "Ask, and ye shall receive." Well, I've been asking for a long time. How long do I have to wait?*

One of the older girls on detail cleaned up the mess. Miss Reutger sent Buster to the cottage and told him to sit in his locker until she got there. I struggled to maintain my balance. If my foot touched the floor, Miss Allen would hit me again. I kept seeing Miss Reutger feeding my baby brother his own vomit and I kept hearing him say, "My thomach hurth."

*Buster, I'm sorry. I didn't mean to lie to you. I really didn't think she would hit you again. I wish I could leave this place and take you with me. We could go some place where people don't beat us and call us names and make us eat vomit.*

I thought about the time I got sick back home. I couldn't remember what was wrong. I just know that I was sick and vomiting all day. Mama put me on the couch in the middle room near the stove and put a bucket on the floor near my head. I remember being very hot, but Mama made me stay under the covers anyway. I had diarrhea and messed up the sheets. Mama cleaned me up and got fresh sheets. She sat beside me on the couch, rubbed my shoulder, and said, "My poor baby. She's so sick." She told me that Daddy would be home soon with some medicine that would make me feel

better. She didn't call me a pig and she didn't hit me.
*Why didn't Miss Reutger just send you to the hospital?*
*She didn't have to hit you. I'm sorry that I made you come*
*back to your table. I should have just took you to the hospi-*
*tal myself. But don't you worry. I'm gonna' remember this.*
*I promise. And I'm gonna' tell.*

I wanted to think about something else, anything but what
had just happened in that dining room. I closed my eyes and
tried to imagine something pleasant; our house on Paisley
Street, a sunset. Even the stench of Daddy's cigars was better than this. I tried to see Mrs. Mart playing arithmetic
games with us. I tried to see Emma and how confused she
was when I tried to teach her Mary Mack the way colored
kids did it back home. I thought of a thousand things to see,
but none of the images lasted more than a few seconds.

Finally, I saw the farmer's son with his turtle—the turtle
that went into its shell to hide from danger. I decided, at that
moment, that I would become a turtle. They would never see
me cry. I wouldn't show any signs of pain. I would just go
inside my shell and I would remember. I would replay every
detail of everything they did to us, just like it was a movie. I
would make a list of what they did and keep it in my head.
And one day, I would tell Betty or Daddy or anybody else
who would listen. I don't know what I expected anybody to
do. I just knew that I had to remember it and I knew that I
had to tell it. And I swore that no matter what they did to us,
they would never see me cry again, not ever.

Our cottage was the last to leave the dining room that
night. When we got to the cottage, none of the girls would
talk to me. We learned early and fast to avoid other kids
when they were in trouble. During devotions, Miss Allen
prayed for me again. She prayed that the Lord would cleanse
me of my evils so I could understand that we were loved;
that she loved me, and Mommy Reutger loved Buster, and
that with love comes discipline. She prayed that I would

understand the value in doing what I was told and that I would learn to keep my big mouth shut.

After prayer, I had to stand and sing a song about a little black sheep that disobeyed its master and got lost. The last line says that "If you only do what you're told to do, you'll always be happy and gay." I hated that song. I was the first and only person in my cottage to sing it. Even I could see, at seven years old, that there was something strange about that: the only colored child in the cottage singing a song about a black sheep who didn't obey his master. If being "happy and gay" meant watching in silence as crazy white people abused innocent children, then I guess I would just be sad and miserable for the rest of my life.

And I was about sick of devotions and the Bible and church. We used to sing a song that says, "God answers prayers in the morning, God answers prayers at noon, God answers prayer in the evening, so keep your heart in tune." *Well, God, why won't you answer my prayers? Isn't my heart in tune? How can I get it in tune so You will listen to me and answer me?*

Buster wasn't in the dining room for breakfast the next morning. I was scared. I thought maybe he vomited at the cottage and Miss Reutger killed him, or maybe eating vomit messed up his insides and he died in his sleep. What, and how was I going to tell Daddy?

When we got to school that day, James told me that they took Buster to the hospital after dinner. He had a stomach virus. He was back in his cottage four days later.

◇

My resolve not to let them see me cry didn't last very long. Near the end of August, the Hollis family came to the Home; Edgar was in Pan 1 and Kevin was in Pan 3. Their little sister, Alison, was in Pan 5. We were all outside playing. Emma, Lauren and I were looking for four-leaf clovers when Alison was introduced to us by her escorts. She was a cute little girl, four years old with blue eyes. She was pale, much more so than the other girls. Her hair was so blonde it was almost white. Both of her brothers were blue-eyed blondes too, though not quite as blonde as Alison was. I was talking to her, asking the usual questions—where are you from, why did you come to the Home—when Edgar yelled to her from the other side of the boundary line. "Alison, get away from her. You know we ain't 'pose to talk to niggers!"

I knew I was suppose to get mad at him, but I didn't. I wasn't a nigger, so it didn't matter to me that he said I was. Some of the kids yelled at him, while others ran to tell. By the time we got to the dining room for dinner, everybody in Peter Pan knew what happened.

We'd been eating for about five minutes when Miss Miller rang her little brass bell and asked Edgar and me to stand. She gave her flower-garden speech again and called him up front. "I know you're new here, but there are some things you need to learn. We don't use words like nigger here at OSSO." As he made his way to her table, she moved her chair to the front of her table. For the first time, we saw the paddle hanging on the back of the chair. It was her big paddle. She had several, but this was the big one—about two feet long and one quarter inch thick with holes in it. She lifted the paddle as she sat. She grabbed Edgar by the wrist and pulled him toward her. "Now I want everybody to see this. This is what happens at OSSO when we use words like nigger." She laid him across her lap and proceeded to beat him. I don't know how many times she hit him. I stopped counting after three.

Edgar was screaming for her to stop. "I'll be good," he sobbed. "I won't say it no more."

"*Any*more. I won't say it *any*more," she said as she continued to hit him.

I didn't want to see this. My ears were ringing from the sound of that paddle whacking against his bottom. My head was pounding from the shrill of his screams. My heart felt as if it would burst and I could feel the tears welling up in my eyes. I thought that if I closed my eyes, the tears would flow back into my head. I squeezed my eyes shut and kept them closed tightly, but it didn't help. I could feel the hot tears stinging my face as they rolled down my cheeks. I tried to go into my shell, but it wasn't deep enough. Alison was crying and so was Kevin, and Edgar just . . . kept. . .screaming!

It seemed to take forever, but it was over in less than a minute. She told Edgar that he owed me an apology. He staggered over to my table and between sobs said, "I'm sorry I called you a nigger."

And as we had been told to do after an apology, I said, "God forgives you, and so do I."

After dinner, Miss Allen called me into her room. "What in the world was wrong with you? Why were you crying?"

We had been getting along fairly well. She really seemed to like me and I liked her. I thought I could tell her the truth. "I didn't want him to get in trouble. It didn't matter that he called me a nigger. I'm not a nigger, so I don't care what he says. If it didn't bother me, then why did Miss Miller get so mad? Why did she beat him like that in front of everybody?"

"My gracious, child, you can't be that stupid. Don't you know that she was defending you, trying to protect your reputation? Don't you have sense enough to see that?"

"I don't know what reputation means."

"Mommy Miller was taking up for you. God doesn't like it when we say hurtful, ugly things to each other. He doesn't like it when we're mean."

I was trying to understand. None of this made sense to me. Tears starting rolling down my face again. And I asked her what I had wanted to know for months. "Does God ever get mad at grown people when they do hurtful, ugly, mean stuff? If God doesn't like it when we're mean, did God like it when Mommy Miller beat Edgar and made us watch? I thought that was mean. Did God like it when Mommy Reutger made my baby brother eat his own vomit? It seems to me that God doesn't like anything we do, and we're just kids."

She just sat there for a moment, slack-jawed, as if she were in shock. When she regained her composure, she back-handed me. And there I was, once again, knocked to the floor for saying something I shouldn't have said.

"Get on your knees, child. We are going to pray. You need to ask the Lord for help and understanding. You need a change of heart and a change of mind. You don't have sense enough to know that Mommy Miller loves you. Don't you know how much it hurts her, and me, when people call you names like that? Nigger. That's such an ugly word. We have to ask the Lord to help you see the light."

She got on her knees and grabbed both of my hands. She squeezed them tight. The harder she prayed, the tighter she squeezed. She prayed as if I were the devil in the flesh; as if I were sinful because I didn't understand, couldn't under-stand how God could punish four-, five-, and six-year-old children for things they did, but ignore the horrible things adults did. When she finished, she told me to take a shower, put on my pajamas, and go straight to bed. "And you'd bet-ter not say one word to anyone."

I wasn't sure if I was to get in the tub or the shower. She said shower, and I was too afraid to ask if she meant bath. I took a shower and went to bed. She must have been really upset with me, because she didn't even want me at devotions.

As soon as I got in bed, I began to sob. I felt like I was going crazy. Nothing made any sense to me anymore. Was I really an evil child, a heathen, incapable of understanding? I was so mad at Miss Miller. I could forgive Edgar for what he said about me, but I would never forgive her for what she did to him. And I would never forgive her for making us watch. I was mad at Miss Allen for always making me feel like the devil. And I was mad at myself for letting her see me cry. I wasn't suppose to cry, not in front of them. That night, I swore on my mother's grave that it would never, ever, happen again. No matter what they did to me or to anyone else, they would never see me cry. Never!

I prayed hard and long. I prayed that this was all a big nightmare and that at any moment, I would wake up in my bed in my house on Paisley Street between Betty and Dean, and that all of this would be over. At 6:20 the next morning, I awoke, still at the Home, still in Pan 6. The nightmare continued.

Ever since the incident with Buster, I hadn't been the same. Sis. Walker noticed the change. I still did my Sunday School homework and still memorized more Bible verses than anyone else, but I was beginning to withdraw, mainly from her. She was, after all, an adult. It was just a matter of time before I asked the wrong question or said the wrong thing that would cause her to beat me and call me names. She had approached me several times to ask what was bothering me. She even asked the minister to talk with me. But I wouldn't talk to either of them. I just kept saying, "Nothing's wrong." I couldn't trust them. I couldn't trust anybody. I had even stopped telling Betty what was happening. Every time I told her something, she would tell Daddy, he'd say something to someone, it got back to Miss Miller and Miss Allen, and I'd get in trouble again. It was an ugly cycle. I finally learned to do what they told us to do. I kept my mouth shut, about some things anyway.

One Sunday after Sunday School, Sis. Walker was sitting near the door, and as I attempted to pass through the doorway, she took my arm. "Come here, baby. Sis. Walker wants to talk to you." She pulled me on her lap and held me close to her bosom. "What's the matter, baby? Why won't you talk to me?"

*Me*, I thought. *Why won't you talk to me?* She hadn't

referred to herself as Sis. Walker. She said *me*. I don't know why, and to this day I haven't figured out why, but something in that simple question—*Why won't you talk to me?*—told me that I could talk to her. The tears flowed freely as I told her everything, about Buster and about Edgar. I told her how Miss Allen tied a diaper on six-year-old Judy Davies and made her wear it outside to play so everybody would know that she had wet the bed. I told her how Barbara had to stand in a corner on one foot for fifteen minutes, because she didn't turn her socks right side out before putting them in the dirty clothes bag. I told her about my doll baby and the prayer circles and how Miss Allen made us feel that we were sinful, dirty, evil children. I told her everything I had seen and heard during the past several months.

Sis. Walker wrapped her big, soft arms around me and held me tighter. I could feel her heart beating against my chest. And as she rocked me back and forth, I thought about my mother. I closed my eyes and was back at 104 Paisley Street. I was outside with Buster and the middle boys, playing in the hot summer sun. We heard the watermelon man calling from down the street. "Watermelons! Strawberries! Pecans!"

Bob said, "Come on. Let's go see."

We ran along the side of the house to the front yard. Mama had told me to keep my sandals on, but I had taken them off anyway. As I neared the front gate, I stepped on something sharp and screamed. Blood gushed from my foot. Bob turned and ran back to me. He looked at my foot and yelled, "Mama! Nancy got a nail in her foot!" He and Bill helped me inside.

Mama sat me on the kitchen table and pulled the nail out. She got a block of ice from the icebox and placed it in a red-trimmed, white enamel-coated bowl, and put my foot on the ice. I cried. It hurt so bad, and the ice made it worse. My leg hurt up to my knee from the cold. And there was just so much blood.

When the bleeding slowed, Mama put some kind of salve on my foot and wrapped it in gauze. She cradled me in her big, soft arms and carried me to the front room and sat me on the couch. She said, "I'll be right back. I got something that'll make you feel better."

She went to the kitchen. I heard the icebox open, then close. She came back with a blue popsicle and sat beside me. She patted her thigh. I climbed on her lap and between sobs, I sucked my popsicle as she rocked me and hummed softly in my ear.

Sis. Walker reached inside her dress and pulled a white hanky from her bosom. She wiped my face. She was so soft and warm, just like Mama. It had been a long time since I felt that safe. I loved Sis. Walker. I wanted her to give me a blue popsicle and tell me everything would be all right. But I wasn't sure a blue popsicle could fix this.

Finally, Sis. Walker spoke. "Baby, baby, baby. I'm sorry. I am so sorry. You are not an evil child. Because a person says a thing doesn't make it so. There are a lot of people who say they're Christians, but their actions say something else. We're just going to have to pray that God will fix their hearts and their tongues and that they will change their ways. But it's going to be all right." She was quiet for a few minutes, then started again. "You can't fix them. You're just a baby. You just do what you're suppose to do, and let God fix the rest. And He can, you know, and believe me, He will."

*When? Why doesn't He do something now? What is He waiting for? It's bad enough that God let Mama die and leave ten kids, including a brand new baby. Then God made us come to the Home, where people who are suppose to take care of us beat us and treat us like dirt. If God could make the whole world, and make the sea open up, and turn water into wine, then God ought to be able to come and take me out of the Home. He ought to be able to make Miss Allen, Miss Miller and the rest of the adults act like human beings, or at least make them treat us as if we are.* I wanted to ask her, "When is God going to fix this? How much longer do I have to wait?"

But I was crying so hard, I couldn't talk any more. Sis. Walker put the hanky in my hand and said, "Here, blow real good. Then Sis. Walker is going to put some water on your face, and we're going upstairs to have church."

◇

In mid-September, Miss Miller had surgery. She was off work for a little over a month. None of the supervisors in Peter Pan had a car, and Miss Miller hadn't made any arrangements for us to get to St. John's. Sunday came and no one knew what to do with us. The supervisors held a quick meeting and decided they'd take us to Emmanuel Baptist Church with the white kids. After all, church was church. How different could they be?

As we got off the big, ugly green buses with the institution's name printed on the side, people stopped and looked at us. The buses weren't new. They had seen those buses every Sunday and were accustomed to them. What they weren't accustomed to, though, was seeing the five colored kids who filed off the buses. There were some gasps and a few strained "hello's", but mostly there were quiet stares as we walked by the silent, Bible-toting Christian white folks who lined both sides of the walk. We followed the other Orphans downstairs for Sunday School. I had just sat down beside Emma when I heard two town girls talking and giggling.

"Ask her," one of them whispered.

"I ain't gonna' ask. You ask her," replied the other.

I knew they were talking about me, but I didn't have any idea what they wanted to know. Finally, the redhead came over to me while the blonde lingered behind. "Um, hi. Um, do you speak English?" she asked.

I didn't answer. She looked back at her friend, who used her Bible to cover her mouth as she laughed. She turned back to me and said, "Why are you here? There's a nigger church up the street." Before I could say anything, she ran back to her friend and they both doubled over with laughter as they ran up the steps.

Emma was furious. "That ole stupid girl. I hope she falls down."

I didn't feel the same way that I felt when Edgar called me a nigger. I honestly believed he just didn't know any better. For some reason, we all had the feeling that these girls knew exactly what they were doing. They were a little older, about eleven or twelve. Besides, they were town kids, so they had to know more than we did.

I didn't like Emmanuel. It was dry and dead, just like chapel. Besides, I didn't feel as if I belonged. I wanted to see Sis. Walker and my friends from Sunday School. I wanted to hear the choir. I wanted to be with people who spoke to me and hugged me and told me how good it was to see me. Other than fellow Orphans, nobody at Emmanuel would even talk to Buster, the Whitaker boys, or me. They would stop talking to each other if we walked by. How we hated that church! I never thought I'd wish for Miss Miller to get well, but I did. I wanted her to take us back to St. John's.

Miss Miller returned after about six weeks. The supervisors told her that things had gone well for us at Emmanuel. I wish she had asked us. We didn't think things had gone very well at all. She called the five of us to her office. She said that since things had gone so smoothly when she was sick, there was no need to upset the apple cart. In other words, we would go to church with the other kids. She said it was "too much trouble to keep making that extra trip."

It wasn't as if Xenia was that big. I could have walked the distance between the two churches in less than fifteen minutes. And I was only seven years old. Besides, she always drove to Emmanuel anyway. She never rode the bus with everybody else. It wouldn't have been that much out of her way to drop us off.

I pleaded with her. "But they're about to start work on the Christmas program. And this year, the boys will have speaking parts and . . ."

She interrupted me. "That's enough. You're going to Emmanuel and that's it."

Paul tried. "But we don't like it there. They don't treat us like they do the other kids. I don't think they like colored people."

She was getting upset. "Now I don't believe that for one minute. Why, I've been going there for years. If they were prejudiced, I'd certainly know it. Maybe it's not them. Maybe it's you. Maybe they think you don't like white people. Did you ever think about that?"

*That's the stupidest thing I ever heard. How could anybody think that? About 600 kids are in the Home and less than 50 of us are colored. Just about everybody we know is white; our teachers, our supervisors, and our friends. Besides, we aren't the ones at Emmanuel calling people names. We aren't the one making fun of people's kinky hair or talking about their flat nose and big lips. We aren't the ones singing about Jesus loving "all the children of the world", and then treating people different because they're colored.*

I tried to change the subject. "Can we at least go say good-bye to our friends?"

She replied, "We'll think about it." That's all I needed to hear. I knew what that meant. Since Mama died, St. John's was the only place I'd been where I felt safe. I didn't want to go to the white church. I wanted to stay where I was wanted, where I was loved, where I belonged.

We would never go to St. John's again, not even to say good-bye. I didn't tell anybody how hurt I was. I went back to my cottage and sat in my locker. I closed my eyes and tried to see Sis. Walker. I wanted to burn her image into my brain so I would always remember what she looked like. I wanted to remember what she smelled like, what she sounded like. I decided to make a memory, to create a moment and freeze it in time. I imagined a wonderful scene of the two of us sitting on a park bench by a duck pond. In my imaginary world, I sat beside her, with my head nestled safely against her bosom, while one of her arms was wrapped securely around my shoulder. The sky was clear, not a cloud anywhere, and the sun was beginning to set. I watched people as they passed by. They would look at us, smile warmly, and continue about their business. We didn't say much of anything. We just sat on the bench, watched the ducks, and ate blue popsicles.

And then, I saw the farmer's son, sitting on the bench with his turtle. And like the turtle, I inched back into my shell and took Sis. Walker with me. I vowed to stay there and never come out again.

# Chapter 8

❦

It was about one week after the school year ended when I moved to Pan 7. Emma and the Johnson twins, June and Jill, moved in about a month later.

The supervisor was Belinda Logan. I thought she and I would get along fine. She, too, was a bit of an outcast, partly because of her looks and partly because of her age. Miss Allen was nearly forty. The other supervisors in Peter Pan were closer to sixty. Belinda was twenty-eight and she was so pretty. Her long black hair hung below her shoulder blades, and she had blue eyes. She was about 5'6" tall and had a nice figure. She wore well-made, stylish clothes, and had a car, a black convertible with lavender leather seats. Some of the supervisors said that she wouldn't last a year.

Miss Logan had been working at the home for about four months when I moved to her cottage. I thought that because she was so new, maybe she didn't know how things were done in Peter Pan; maybe she might be a little nicer.

She was from a close family, who lived in Xenia, so they came to visit her a lot. She had two older brothers, Peter and Richard, and three younger siblings, Catherine, Krystal and

Vinnie. It was Krystal and Vinnie who initially endeared the family to us and us to them. Krystal was two years older than we were and Vinnie was our age. When they visited her, they spent time with us.

Krystal and Vinnie were really nice, and that surprised us. Our experiences with town kids were not very pleasant. They played tricks on us and teased us about everything from our hair to our shoes. If they were nice, it was part of a set up or they just wanted to verify rumors they'd heard about the Home. We were the poor, pitiful little orphans that nobody wanted. But Krystal and Vinnie weren't like that. They would talk to us and play with us. And they didn't treat me any differently from the other girls. It didn't matter to them that I was colored. With town kids, I could never be sure, but I was sure about them.

Belinda's parents encouraged us to call them Grandma and Grandpa. They didn't make us do it; they gave us a choice. I never knew my grandparents. Both of my father's parents and my mother's father were dead before I was born. My mother's mother died when I was three. So I thought it was neat to finally have some grandparents. Most of us were so starved for love and kindness that we would have claimed as family anybody who was nice to us.

Grandma and Grandpa Logan treated us all as if we really were their grandchildren. They would come into the play-room and get on the floor with us and color or play jacks and pick-up sticks. They read to us and let us read to them. They would tell stories as we sat on their laps. They wanted to know about school and what subjects we liked, which ones we didn't. They asked about our families and our friends. They were genuinely nice people. And sometimes they brought treats, usually Circus Peanuts or Mary Janes. We always had a good time with them.

The Logan family sang as a group in their church. Sometimes they would sing to us on their visits. They had such wonderful, strong voices, and the harmony was beautiful. I particularly liked Richard's voice, especially when he sang lead on *"How Great Thou Art."*

I had a major crush on Richard. He was so handsome. Like the rest of his family, he was dark, with black hair, and the clearest blue eyes and the warmest smile. And though his hands were large, they were very gentle. I don't really know if Richard could sing any better or worse than the rest of his family. I just know that whatever Richard did was tops in my book.

Jill and I started calling each other "in-law." She was in love with Peter. He was a few years younger than Richard. We called him "Uncle Peach Tree." He was so long, about 6'3" tall and rail thin. Like Richard, he had those blue eyes and black hair and a voice as smooth as satin. Jill was determined that one day she would marry him. And I knew, as sure as I knew that I was colored, that one day, I would marry Richard.

So imagine our devastation when we went to a park in town for a picnic with the entire family and Peter and Richard announced their engagements. Jill looked at me with her mouth wide open, then looked at Peter, and took off running. She ran down by Massie's Creek and sat by a large maple tree. Grandpa went after her and tried to find out what was wrong. I don't remember if she told him or not, but I knew what it was. Her heart was shattered. She felt as if someone had just kicked her in the stomach. Her head was spinning. She was mad at Peter. She was mad at his fiancé and she was jealous. She hadn't told me, but I knew. I felt the same way about Richard. I just couldn't—wouldn't let everybody know it. I wouldn't talk to Richard; in fact, I shut down completely. I wouldn't talk to anyone. And I wouldn't play or eat. I just sat on the ground with my knees drawn tightly to my chest and watched little brown ants scurrying back to their anthill with crumbs of food.

When we got back to the cottage, we showered and had devotions. When we went to bed, the family came into the dormitory and sang to us. I lay on my stomach and cried quietly. I knew Jill was crying too. Though several of the girls knew how Jill felt about Peter, she was the only one who knew how I felt about Richard. Jill and I became a lot closer after that. We had so much in common—unrequited love—at seven years old.

◇

Every year during the Fourth of July weekend, the Home held a reunion. Ex-pupils came back to campus from all over the country. Some of the Exes hadn't missed a reunion in twenty or thirty years. What an exciting time that was.

On Reunion Saturday, all the kids in Peter Pan went to the parade field. The Exes organized games and activities for us. I didn't like the sack race very much, but I loved the three-legged race. I don't think I was ever a part of a winning team because one of us always fell. But I didn't care. To me, falling down was part of the fun in a three-legged race.

The relay races were fun too. Sometimes each cottage would pick a team of four or six, and we competed against other cottages. Sometimes, it was boys against girls. And it never mattered who won. The Exes gave everybody a ribbon.

And they'd have a money hunt. The supervisors passed out paper bags while several of the Exes would throw candy, wrapped in clear paper all over the parade field. Inside some of the wrappers, they had placed pennies, nickels, and dimes. We stood, anxiously, in a large circle. One of the men would yell, "On your mark, get set, go!" We ran and screamed like banshees. We gathered as much candy as we could within the time limit. When the hunt was over, we sat and scanned each piece of candy, searching for the coins inside. Whoever had the most money got a dollar.

After the organized games, sometimes we'd stay on the main campus for a while and play with the children of the

Exes. Most of them were really nice to us and we had a lot of fun. To them, we weren't orphans who were to be pitied. We were just kids. And we had something in common with their parents.

On the way back to Peter Pan, we stopped on the boys' side for the softball game, Exes against the Orphans. The Orphans usually won. Many of the Exes may have been lettermen when they were in the Home, but the Orphans were still winning state championships in just about every sport. Time had taken its toll on these former athletes. They were simply out classed.

I hadn't seen Betty or Dean for a long time, except for our occasional visits with Daddy or Miss Jenkins. Their visits weren't as regular as I would have liked.

We were on our way to school one day. Dean was running late. The rest of her cottage had already gone. As she ran across the street, she saw me walking with my cottage and stopped beside me. "Hi Nancy," she said.

I looked at her and shook my head.

"What's the matter with you? I said hi."

I shook my head again and whispered, "We can't talk."

By now, she was getting mad. "What do you mean you can't talk?"

"Sssshhhh!" Now I was getting mad. Not only was she going to be in trouble for talking to me, but I would be in trouble too. Everybody would know that I had talked to her.

Miss Miller came up behind Dean and said, "Young lady, go on to school. You're not to be with this group."

Dean stopped and looked at her. "This is my little sister. I can talk to her if I want to."

"No you may not. Now get away from her." She pushed Dean. "Go on to your class and mind your own business."

Dean looked at me. I guess the urgency of my expression was enough to tell her not to say anything else. She ran to the building and turned as she neared the door. "I hate you, you big fat jackass!" she yelled to Miss Miller.

That night, Miss Miller came to our cottage after devotions. She reiterated the incident for the entire cottage, although they were there and saw and heard everything. She said that we needed to "pray for Bernadine Gibson. She is an evil child, a child of the devil, and she needs salvation."

All I heard was that my dead mother was the devil. I lost my mind. I screamed at her. "My mama ain't no devil, and my sister ain't no devil child neither." She came across the room and slapped me so hard, my nose started bleeding. She refused to let me get a tissue or a wash cloth. Instead, she called for a prayer circle and dragged me to the center. She prayed, not only for my soul, but also for Dean's. She asked the Lord to "help these evil children", at which point I interrupted her prayer.

"Why do you keep saying that? We haven't seen each other in a long time. All she did was speak to me. What's so evil about that?"

I could feel the fear and tension in the air. Miss Miller sent the other girls to bed without finishing her prayer. They didn't even go through the hug and kiss routine. She told Belinda to bring the paddle. And then she started yelling at me and pushing me. She called me evil, and other things that I didn't understand; belligerent, defiant, rebellious, and more than I can remember.

Belinda returned with the paddle and handed it to Miss Miller. She stood there, expressionless, as Miss Miller beat me, almost as badly as she had beaten Edgar Hollis. The difference was that I would not cry, and I would not beg her to stop. I just stood there, clenching my teeth, waiting for it to end.

She continued to yell at me. "Something is very wrong with you. You've been in Peter Pan long enough to know how things are done, and you still don't get it. You refuse to obey the rules. You still want things done your way. Well, that is not going to happen, young lady. I control Peter Pan. I control everything that happens in Peter Pan. Where you go, when you go, when you talk, if you talk, what you do, and when you do it. And you will learn, even if I have to beat it into you."

She had the power. As far as she was concerned, she controlled everybody and everything in Peter Pan. But I knew better. There were some things she couldn't control. As hard as she might try, she couldn't control what I thought or felt. And she couldn't control whether or not I cried. As much as I wanted to cry, and as much as she wanted to see me cry, she couldn't control that. And I was determined that I would not cry. She would not break me. None of them would.

I stood there and looked at her and thought, *You are a hateful, ugly woman. When Edgar called me a nigger, you took up for me by beating him. I take up for my sister, and you beat me. No matter what we do, we're always wrong. Are you ever wrong, Miss Miller? Who beats you when you do the wrong thing or say the wrong thing? My sister is not evil and neither am I. If anybody is evil, it's you, you evil, hateful, ugly witch!*

She called Belinda over for another prayer. As she walked toward us, she wouldn't look at me. I couldn't believe she stood there and watched the whole thing. I don't know what I expected her to do or why I expected her to do anything, but I didn't think she would just stand there and watch!

We got on our knees as Miss Miller again prayed that God would "touch my evil spirit and cleanse my filthy heart." When she finished, she sent me to get a bucket and a rag to clean my blood off the floor. After I emptied the bucket, I washed my face and changed my pajamas and went back to the playroom.

As I entered the room, she stretched out her arms. I went to her and completed the meaningless ritual. She kissed my cheek and said, "Good night, honey. Mommy Miller loves you."

I kissed her and said, "Good night, Mommy Miller." As I walked toward the door, I said, "Good night, Mommy Belinda." I didn't kiss her, I didn't look at her. I didn't wait for a response. I just kept walking.

I don't know what punishment, if any, Dean got, but I lost all my privileges for two weeks. I could only go to school, church, and the dining room. I had to sit in the playroom and watch through the window as the other girls played outside. When they played inside, I had to sit on my cubbie and watch them. They couldn't talk to me during playtime, and I couldn't talk to them. If they got a treat, I had to sit and watch them eat it, knowing I couldn't have any because "I was an evil child." They didn't like eating in front of me anymore than I liked eating in front of Miss Patrick's class. There wasn't a girl in that cottage who, under normal circumstances, wouldn't have shared anything she had with anybody. Though I knew they would have, I also knew they couldn't. These were not normal circumstances. And I was beginning to think that there was absolutely nothing normal about anything at the OS&SO Home. Or, there was absolutely nothing normal about me!

Things were different between Belinda and me after that. I could tell that she was no different from the other supervisors. And after a while, it affected the way I interacted with her family. They didn't treat me any differently, though. Eventually, I warmed up to them again, but my relationship with Belinda would never be the same.

One day, and I don't know why, I decided that I couldn't call her "Mommy" anymore. It was a normal day. We went to school. We came home and played. We had dinner, and showered and had devotions. Then we went to the dormitory.

As was the practice, we stood at the foot of our beds and, starting in the far corner, we said, "Good night, Mommy

Belinda" then jumped into bed with the precision of the Rockettes. The first seven or eight girls went through the routine as usual, then it was my turn. I said, "Good night, Miss Logan" and jumped into bed.

The girls let out a collective gasp, and stared at me with wide-eyed amazement. "What did you call me?" she demanded.

"Miss Logan," I answered.

She started across the room. "Get out of that bed." I got up and stood at the foot of my bed. She hovered over me with her hands on her hips. "Do you want to try that again?" she asked.

I looked up into her eyes. There was an icy coldness in those clear blue eyes that I had never seen before. I said it again, slowly and deliberately. "Good night, ... Miss . . . Logan."

She hit me so hard I fell backward, half on the bed and half on the floor. I struggled to get up. She grabbed my arm and pushed me toward the door. "You go to your locker and wait for me."

Some of the girls started crying. They knew what was about to happen. After they finished the ritual, Belinda went to her room. I sat in my locker, in the dark. Though it seemed like a very long time, it was probably about fifteen minutes. She came out of her room and walked slowly to the playroom. A few minutes later, she called for me. As I walked down the hall, I could see her pacing. She held a paddle in her hand.

"Why did you call me Miss Logan?"

"Because that's your name."

"You are suppose to call me Mommy Belinda."

"But why? You're not my mother."

"I don't care. You know the rules. You are to call me Mommy Belinda."

"But I don't understand. Why do I have to call you

Mommy? My mother is dead. Besides, you couldn't be my mother. I'm colored and you're white."

She whacked me across the thigh with the paddle. "You have a lot to learn, young lady. And you will learn. You will do exactly what you're told and when you're told. Enough of this silliness." She took me by the arm, spun me around and began to paddle me. After the first couple of whacks, she asked, "What is my name?"

"Miss Logan," I replied.

She continued to hit me, pausing periodically to ask me her name. Each time my answer was the same—"Miss Logan." She didn't hit nearly as hard as Miss Miller, though she did get in a couple of good licks. And unlike with Miss Miller, I didn't even want to cry. But I had to pee. I was having trouble holding it. I was afraid that if she hit me again, she would literally knock the pee out of me. I don't know how many times she hit me. So when she asked again, "What's my name?", I finally answered, "Mommy Belinda."

Her expression changed from anger to smug, self-satisfaction. I suppose that was some type of victory for her. She thought she had broken a seven-year old child. The reality was, I had to *go* and I couldn't wet my pants. "I have to number one. Can I go?"

"*May I,*" she said as she pointed to the door.

I hurried past her and down the hall. *Hold it. Hold it. Don't pee in your pants!* I was almost running. *Hurry! You're almost there. Oh, I made it.* As I sat on the toilet, I wondered, *Why do I have to call her Mommy? Why won't anybody answer that? She is not my mother. My mother was a colored woman named Ellen Gibson and she's dead. Why do I have to call these white women Mommy?*

I understood how things were done in Peter Pan. I understood how things were done at the OS&SO Home. I just didn't understand why. If something didn't make sense, I would ask. More times than not, I got in trouble for it. Kids got in trouble for far less, so I figured I had nothing to lose. When I returned, she reached out and hugged me. Her voice cracked with emotion as she told me how much she loved me. "I love all of you girls. It hurts me when you act like this. It makes me sad and it makes Jesus sad. I love you, Nancy, and I wish you wouldn't make me hit you." She kissed my cheek and sent me to bed.

I walked toward the dormitory. *She beats me because she loves me. Miss Miller beats me because she loves me. Mama said she loved me, but she never beat me. Do love and beatings go together? Miss Jenkins said she loved us. In the six months we lived with her, she never beat us or tried to make us call her Mama. Now that Mama is dead, I love Buster more than anybody or anything in the world. Maybe I'm suppose to beat him up so he will know how much I love him. And I love Emma too. She's my best friend. Maybe I should beat her up too.*

I crawled into bed and pulled the sheet over my head. I was so confused. *I make Jesus sad. Then why doesn't God do something? Maybe God can tell me why I have to call her Mommy. Maybe He can help me understand why these people are so mean and make us do stupid stuff for no reason. Then maybe I can be quiet and stop asking questions that get me in trouble so nobody will have to beat me and then Jesus won't be sad anymore.* Then it dawned on me. *Maybe God thinks I'm a devil child too! Maybe that's why He won't do anything.*

I was awake for a long time trying to figure out what I could do differently, how I could fix what was wrong with me. Being white was out of the question. I couldn't do that. Besides, it wouldn't make any difference. White kids got beat all the time too. Quiet conformity never crossed my mind. I couldn't come up with anything. So, I just lay there until I finally drifted off to sleep.

◇ ◇ ◇

# Chapter 9

✣

I was transferred to Taylor B, the junior campus, just before the third grade. I'd be with Miss Allen again. The Yengers, the only couple who served as supervisors, had resigned and Miss Allen was transferred to Taylor.

The layout in Taylor was different from the other cottages in Peter Pan. It was newer and brighter and had large picture windows. We had a dormitory, like the other cottages, but it was a lot bigger. And we had dressers and closets. But what I liked best was that the toilet stalls had doors that closed and locked, and the shower and the tub had curtains.

Bootsie was already there. I liked her, but at the same time, I resented her. She was colored too, and about six months younger than I. She came to the Home during the second grade. She went straight to Taylor, while the rest of us were in Pan 7. Age, grade and seniority usually were considered when cottage assignments were made. In Bootsie's case, none of those things seemed to matter. We got along well in school, but I wasn't sure how it would be to live together.

In the first and second grades, all of us had the same teacher all the time. But in the third grade, they divided us into two groups. Group I was suppose to be the smart kids, and was assigned to Mrs. Patrick. Group II was the "not-so-smart" kids, and was assigned to Miss Pennington. Bootsie and I were both in Group I. Emma, Jill and Lauren were in Group II. I didn't like that. They were as smart as anybody else was and I couldn't figure out how it was decided who was smart and who wasn't. Of course, I didn't ask anybody.

Both Mrs. Patrick and Miss Pennington decided that we would perform a play, *The Land of Dreams Come True*, that would involve both groups of third graders. It was to be a major production, so the high school drama teacher would direct it. Usually, when the elementary grades performed a play, it was only for the elementary school during the regular school day. This was to be at night for the entire Home. This was a big deal!

Julian Robert Rooney was the drama teacher. Most of the kids called him JR, with his permission. I couldn't do that, so I always called him Mr. Rooney. He met with us to discuss the play. The high school stagecraft class would build and paint the set, work the lights and curtain, and help with make-up and costumes. After the third or fourth meeting, he chose the cast. Bootsie was to play the Mother Goose, and I was to play the Old Woman In The Shoe. They were both large roles. At first, I was excited about it. But when I saw the script and realized how much I had to learn, I was scared. I was afraid to tell him that I didn't think I could do it. Mr. Rooney had a reputation for having a short fuse. And, like the rest of the adults, he didn't want anyone to question his decisions. But I didn't see any sense in waiting until the last minute to tell him, so after about the second rehearsal, I told him.

"Um, Mr. Rooney, I can't do this part. It's too big. There are way too many lines."

He squatted on the floor in front of me. He placed his hands on my shoulders and said, "Yes you can. You may not think so, but I do. Trust me. You'll be great." He smiled, patted my shoulder, and got up.

I wanted to believe him. I wanted to trust somebody. He was the first adult since Sis. Walker that I even thought about trusting. For some unknown reason, I needed to believe in him, and I needed to believe that he believed in me. So I made the decision, a very difficult decision, to trust Mr. Rooney. I did everything he told me to do without question, and eventually, without fear. I watched his every move and listened to every inflection. I was his echo and his shadow.

Bootsie and I ran lines together in the cottage. The play helped us become much closer. We had so many lines to learn and a lot of scenes together. We each wanted the other to look good.

Opening night arrived and we were petrified. We didn't think we could go on. Micky Maxwell had a headache. Jill had a stomach ache. Emma had a sore throat. Bootsie's leg hurt, and Barbara had every ache in the book. And I thought I was going to faint. We were scared and didn't know what to do. Mr. Rooney came into the dressing room. "Are we about ready to go on?"

We just looked at each other, afraid to say anything. Finally, Barbara said, "We can't go on, Mr. Rooney. I think we have the flu or food poisoning or something. Everybody is sick."

He smiled. "Oh, that's just stage fright. Once you get on stage, you'll be all right."

I thought, *Man, are you dense? Didn't you just hear what she just said? She said we can't go on!*

She said it again, "But we're sick. We can't do it."

I finally blurted out, "We're scared."

He said, "Yes, I know you are. But if you do everything we rehearsed, exactly as we rehearsed it, you will be fine. Just pretend that this is another rehearsal and that nobody is out there except me. I'll be standing in the back. When it's time to look into the audience, look at me. You won't be able to see my face, but you'll know it's me. I'll be the only one standing in the center aisle. Now let's get in places and let's have a good show."

We filed out of the dressing room and got in place for our entrances. We stood in the wings and trembled. I was more nervous than I had ever been. I heard my cue and walked out on stage. I said my lines and the audience roared with laughter. It caught me by surprise. I knew the line was suppose to be funny, but I didn't think it was *that* funny. I did as Mr. Rooney had told me: I waited until they stopped laughing before I continued.

We cooked! The first act was over in no time. Mr. Rooney ran back stage. He was grabbing, hugging, patting, or kissing everybody. "They love you guys! You are just great! And I thought you couldn't do this show." We all smiled. He continued, "Now listen. Check your props for Act II. I want you to go out there and do the same thing that you did in Act I."

We all just stood there for a minute, grinning at each other, wondering what we had done that was so fantastic. Whatever it was, we just wanted to do it again. And we did. Act II was better than Act I. We got a standing ovation and two curtain calls.

After everybody left the theatre, Mr. Rooney called us on stage. He told us how wonderful we were and how much he enjoyed working with us. "I expect to see some of you in my drama class when you reach high school. Thanks, guys, for a great show. Now go on and change your clothes so you can get out of here."

For a second, I thought he was going to cry. I felt an overwhelming urge to hug him, so I ran to him and threw my arms around his waist. "Thank you for helping us, Mr. Rooney." I didn't wait for a response. I took off running toward the dressing room.

Miss Allen came back stage to help us change clothes.

As we were leaving for the cottage, she told me Mr. Rooney wanted to talk to me. "We'll wait for you in the lobby," she said.

*Why does he want to talk to me? What did I do? Did I drop lines or step on somebody else's lines? Did I miss a cue? Did I upstage somebody?* I couldn't think of anything I had done wrong.

I walked out on stage Mr. Rooney was sitting in the first row in the auditorium. He had something white in his hands. As I neared the bottom of the steps, he reached for me. I walked into his arms. "You've got it, kiddo. I don't think you know it. I'm not sure anybody else sees it either, but I do. You were really great tonight."

"Thank you, Mr. Rooney."

"So, you are going to major in drama, right?"

"I don't know," I replied. I hadn't really thought about it. I was only in the third grade. I couldn't major until the ninth grade, so it wasn't anything that had crossed my mind.

"I'd love to have you in my class. You're a natural. If ever anybody belonged on stage, you do. Here. I want you to have this." He handed me the white cloth, which, as it turned out, was the nightcap I had worn in the show. It was unheard of for us to keep props or costumes.

"Really? I can have it? For keeps?"

"For keeps. Now go on and catch up with your cottage."

"Thank you, Mr. Rooney." As I ran up the aisle, I stuffed the cap in my pocket and shouted over my shoulder. "I'll be in your drama class in six more years. Bye."

When we got back to the cottage, I showed the nightcap to Miss Allen. She remarked how generous Mr. Rooney was to have given it to me, but the Christian thing for me to have done was reject the cap in case it could be used in another show. The next day, I had to take the cap back to school and give it to Mr. Rooney. I really hated to do that. I wanted to keep it, though I really didn't need it. Mr. Rooney

105

had given me so much more than a white, cotton nightcap. He had given me something that I didn't ever have to give back, something that would stay with me for the rest of my life. Mr. Rooney believed in me. That was the most wonderful feeling, the most wonderful gift. And nobody, not Miss Allen, not Miss Miller, not anybody at the OS&SO Home or anywhere else in the world could ever take that away from me.

◇

The main campus was still segregated. Taft B had lost several girls while I was in Peter Pan. Some had graduated and some left early. Though a lot of white girls had come to the Home, very few colored girls came during my Peter Pan years.

In May, just before the end of the third grade, I was told I was moving back to campus. I was overjoyed. Although I'd miss my friends, especially Emma, Lauren, Jill, and Boostie, I'd still see them in school. Besides, within a year or two, most of them would be on campus anyway. I was going back to Taft with Mrs. Vincent. She was dry and stern, and could be a little grouchy at times, but she was never mean. She had never hit me or called me names or broken my toys.

And I would be with my sisters again. I hoped we could still share a room. It would be good to see them every day. And I'd get to see my brothers, at least in the dining room. I hated to leave Buster. I would miss him, but I would not miss Peter Pan.

Some of the girls were jealous. There were at least eight, maybe ten girls in Taylor who were older than I was. Technically, they should have gone to campus first. But, there was an open slot for a colored girl on the main campus. There were now about five colored girls in Peter Pan and I was the oldest, so I was at the top of the list.

About two weeks after school was out, Mrs. Vincent came to get me. Patsy Billings and Peggy O'Shea helped me carry my boxes. I was upset with Miss Allen about that. I liked Patsy and Peggy, but they were not among my closest friends. She could have let Emma, Bootsie, Jill, or Lauren help me carry my belongings. But she knew that's what I would have wanted, so, naturally, she wouldn't do that.

Patsy and Peggy had never seen the inside of the cottages on campus. Most of the kids in Peter Pan hadn't. They were astounded at the fact that there were no dormitories. I had told them that when I first went to Peter Pan. I guess they didn't believe me.

As soon as Patsy and Peggy left, Mrs. Vincent came into the room and started marking my clothes again. As she had done the first time, she asked me what fit and what didn't. I didn't have to strip or try on my underwear. She reminded me about wearing my housecoat over my pajamas whenever I left my room at night. She gave me more socks and ordered a few other items she thought I should have and that was it.

Betty had moved upstairs with the "big" girls. Jackie Whitaker was still downstairs, and shared the big room, our old room, with Bootsie's sisters, Marci and JoAnne. Dean was still downstairs too, and we shared a room. She had changed a lot since I had moved to Peter Pan. We didn't seem to have much in common anymore and didn't have as much fun as we used to.

Betty, on the other hand, just didn't seem to have time for me any more. She was a teenager, and like most teenaged girls, she didn't want her little sister hanging around all the time. She was busy with her friends and it seemed that I was in the way. I started making new friends.

Junie Bivins and Darlene Thomas were already on campus. They were in my grade, but had never been in Peter Pan. Many of the older white girls who had befriended me earlier were still there. Even though they were five and six years older than I was, they became my friends.

There was a new minister on campus. His name was Rev.

Hargrave. He was more relaxed than Rev. White. All the kids called him Rev. Although Rev. White was dry and dull, he was a nice man. I was a little disappointed that he was gone. I wasn't sure I'd like Rev. Hargrave. I'd just have to wait and see.

# Chapter 10

ॐ

I was in Miss Peters' class for fourth grade. That was the year I had my first boyfriend. In the third grade, I had a short-lived crush on Carl Bronson. He and James were the only colored boys in my grade. Carl had come to the Home around the middle of the third grade, and he was so tall and so cute. He was among our small group of third-grade swimmers who played in the deep end of the pool. There were so few of us that we became fast friends. Junie Bivins and I were the only girls. Carl, Bobby Wade, and Chuck Martin made up the rest of the group. Carl never gave the slightest indication that he liked me. It would be many years later when I learned that Carl had a crush on me too.

Micky Maxwell was in the Home when I got there. He was one of the cutest boys in my class. All the girls liked him. He had very blonde hair and blue eyes. He had freckles on his nose and a few on his cheeks. He had the whitest teeth I had ever seen. And they were so perfect, not a gap, a chip, or a cavity anywhere.

We were hanging up our coats one day, when he turned to me and said, "Nancy, will you go with me?" I was shocked.

My mouth fell open and I could feel the warmness of a blush ascending my face. "Yea," I answered. "O.K.," he said. "You're my girlfriend." As the other kids hung up their coats, we held hands while Barbara Larson acted as look-out in case Miss Peters came along.

By the time we returned from lunch that afternoon, all the kids in class knew about Micky and me. Several of the girls came up to me. "Did Micky Maxwell really ask you to go with him?" "Oh, you're so lucky." "You guys make a cute couple." It wasn't as if we knew what "going together" really meant. It was just something to say, and made us feel very grown up.

The next day in music class, Emma told me she saw Micky wink at Junie. I got mad. "Do you like Junie Bivins?" I demanded to know.

"I think she's kind of cute," he replied.

"Well," I said. "If you think she's so cute, you can just go with her. It's quits." My first boyfriend lasted less than twenty-four hours. The next day, he asked Junie to go with him. She, of course, said yes. They went together for two days. Micky went with most of the girls in our class that year. None of the unions lasted more than two or three days. Some didn't even make it to lunch. So much for young love.

◇

We all took Flutophone lessons during the fourth grade. That was to prepare us for instrument selection at the end of the year. I was pretty good at it. I didn't learn to read music, but I soon discovered that I could play anything I heard. Mr. Showalter was the band teacher, and he would come to the elementary side of the building to work with us. He was impressed with my musical ear; however, my inability to read music was a constant source of frustration for him.

At the end of the year, he came down for the instrument selection process. When my turn came, I said I wanted to play the drums. He was agitated. "The drum is a boy's instrument, not a girl's. Now quit being silly and tell me what you want to play or I'll make an assignment."

I wasn't being silly. I wanted to play the drums. I didn't understand the difference between a boy's instrument and a girl's instrument. Peggy Galvin played the saxophone. She was the only girl I knew who did. Wasn't that a boy's instrument? I wasn't about to ask him that. So I said that I wanted to play the harp. There was a beautiful harp in the band room that I had never seen anyone play. When we saw orchestras on television, it was always a woman who played the harp. I thought, *Surely, the harp is a girl's instrument.*

He told me neither he nor Mr. Cooke could teach the harp. I didn't know why not. He taught everything except piano and strings. Mr. Cooke taught those. How much more difficult could it be to teach the harp. I wondered if they couldn't teach it or if they just didn't want to teach it to me. I didn't ask him that either. I simply said I'd to play the piano. Finally, something on which we could agree.

The Home owned a camp in Clifton, Camp Cooper, about five or six miles outside of Xenia. We went to camp every summer, in groups of about 50, for a week at a time. I liked camp. Every day, if it didn't rain, we'd go for a hike. At least once during our week-long stay, we took an all-day hike of about six-to-eight miles.

The older girls served as cabin counselors. Miss Williams, the girls' gym teacher, supervised camp for the girls. That year, our cabin chose Cedarville for the all-day hike. I don't remember how long it took, but it seemed like ten hours. It was probably close to an hour and a half. We rested on the campus of Cedarville College. We each had a sack lunch, which consisted of a peanut butter and jelly sandwich, a hard-boiled egg, a dill pickle, and two oatmeal-raisin cookies. We rested under a large tree near a water fountain. Some of us didn't have the dime it cost to buy a bottle of pop. Those who did, shared theirs. Like winos on a street corner, we passed the bottles from one to another until everybody had a sip. And when we were finished, we returned the bottles for the deposit, pooled our change, and bought another bottle.

We were almost half way back to camp when Miss Williams came along in her green station wagon. The very white girls, blondes and redheads, were told to get in the car. They were beginning to burn. Junie and I had to get in too. We were the youngest girls at camp at age ten. Miss Williams thought that hike was a bit much for us. We both wanted to hike with the rest of the cabin to prove that we were big girls. Though, I must say, once Miss Williams started that car and the breeze came through those windows and the tailgate, I was happy for the ride.

Every night after dinner, we had some organized activity: softball, volleyball, tin-can-Johnny, treasure hunts, or scavenger hunts. I didn't enjoy softball much, but everything else was fun, especially the treasure hunts. On the last night, we had a talent show. It was also prank night, when we played tricks on our counselors. They would go to the mess hall or stay in the shelter house while we went to the cabins and did whatever we were going to do. We'd short-sheet their beds, hide their underwear or toothbrushes, and sometimes, we didn't do anything at all. The expectation of doom was often worse than the doom itself.

The last day at camp was always sad. We had so much fun that we didn't want to go back to the Home. After breakfast, we'd load our boxes on the bus and head back to the campus. As we neared the gates, someone started singing, "We're here, because we're here," to the tune of Auld Lang Syne. We all joined in. Then somebody started crying, and pretty soon, most of us were crying. We were a sensitive group. Whatever one felt—joy, sorrow, pain—we all did. Camp was a time when we all could relax and have a good time. Even Miss

Williams seemed nicer when we were at camp.

When we returned from camp that summer, I got the surprise of my life. They, whoever they were, had decided to integrate the main campus. Marci and I were being transferred to Garfield A. We should have gone to Jefferson A, but Miss Jackson, the supervisor, refused to have any "niggers" in her cottage.

There were two supervisors named Bennett; one in Jackson B and one in Garfield A. To avoid confusion, the one in Garfield was called Miss B. She was no better than Miss Jackson.

Two girls in Garfield didn't have roommates, Roxanne Duncan and Pam Streeter. Miss B asked Marci and me which of us wanted to room with Roxanne. Since Marci was much quieter than I was, I waited for her to answer first. When she didn't say anything, I said I would.

Roxanne was at band practice when we moved in. It didn't take long to settle in, and we were taking our daily nap when she returned to the cottage. I had seen her around campus, but didn't really know her. She was one of Dean's good friends.

Roxanne was a bit of a tomboy. She was an Elvis Pressley fan, and her thick, dark hair was cut in a ducktail like his. She had blue eyes and dimples. She was smart and very athletic and could run faster and hit a baseball further than just about anybody, including a lot of the boys. She was a cheerleader, too, and could jump higher and better than most of the other girls. And she was really popular.

When she came into the room, I was still awake. She said, "Oh, so you're my new roomie. Let me tell you a few things you need to know."

I thought, *Oh boy, I guess she's the queen bee in this cottage.*

She continued. "Most of the girls aren't sure how this integration thing is going to work. They don't think it will be a problem though, 'cause we already go to school with you guys. But Miss B doesn't like colored people. She can be real nasty and mean. If you ever have any problems with her, you let me know. Want some candy?"

"Sure," I said.

She gave me a piece of her Zero bar and plopped on her bed. I had a feeling that I would like Roxanne and that I would like being her roommate. Marci didn't say much one way or the other about rooming with Pam. But they seemed to get along fine.

Roxanne's good friend was Yvette Dixon, but everybody called her Cricket. I had been in the cottage about three months when Roxanne and Cricket decided to sneak out after hours. I asked to go with them, but Roxanne didn't want me to. She and Cricket were nearly five years older than I was, and they didn't think I could keep up with them. Besides, they didn't think I could deal with the punishment if we got caught. I convinced them that I would be fine and the plan was put in motion.

Miss Hankins was one of several white relief supervisors. It seemed that whenever Miss B was off, we always got stuck with Miss Hankins. Behind her back, we called her "Old Hawkear". She was known for her proclamation that, "I can hear a flea land on a dog." When Miss Hankins was on duty, no one ever tried to sneak out.

Roxanne and Cricket decided she bragged a little too much. They were going to test her and see just how good her hearing really was. We waited until about 10:30. We stuffed our beds with pillows and stuffed animals and tiptoed down the hall, down the steps, and out the back door.

First, we went to the apple orchard. We sat in the trees and ate Granny Smith apples and talked and laughed and had a good time. The window to the hayloft of the barn was open. Roxanne decided we should have a contest to see if we could throw apples through the window without hitting the side of the barn. I wasn't very successful at that. The cows were going crazy. We could hear them mooing and moving. The farmers couldn't figure out what was upsetting them so. Every so often, the farmers came out of the barn and looked around but didn't see anything or anybody.

After we stuffed a laundry bag full of apples, we headed to the football field. Roxanne wanted to climb a goal post, swing hand-over-hand across the crossbeam, and slide down the other post. While she made her way up the post, Cricket and I ran around the track. Cricket, was heavy and bow-legged and didn't run very fast or very far. She stopped half way through the first lap. As she collapsed on the football field, she whispered, "Chickie! Chickie! The cops! The cops!" We looked up and in the distance, we could see the night watchman's flashlight.

Roxanne whispered, "Don't move. Just be real still."

So, there she was, hanging from the cross-beam of the goal post, Cricket, collapsed in a lump in the middle of the football field, and me standing on the track, with my arms outstretched like the branches of a tree. The beam of the watchman's light was shining on Roxanne's chest. We knew we were in big trouble. For about thirty seconds, we didn't breathe or move. The light traveled down the length of her body and suddenly went out. He turned and walked in the opposite direction.

Roxanne dropped from the goal post and said, "Let's get out of here."

Cricket said, "Wait. The hurdle."

They grabbed a hurdle and I grabbed the apples and we ran back to the cottage. We put the hurdle under my bed, dropped our clothes and climbed into bed. We made it out and back without Miss Hankins knowing it, and we had a laundry bag of apples and a hurdle to prove it.

The next morning as we left for breakfast, we were sure we were caught. The grass on the football field had been cut on the day we were out. We had tracked wet grass in the cottage, up the steps, down the hall, and into our rooms. Miss Hankins didn't even notice it.

I left the dining room early to go to the hospital to take medicine for an ear infection. I ran to the cottage first, got the hurdle, and walked across the campus, in broad daylight, dragging a hurdle behind me, and not a soul stopped me to ask why. I put the hurdle on the steps of the Armory and continued on to the hospital.

By lunch, half the girls' side knew of our exploits. We were really hot stuff. What we couldn't figure out, though, was why the night watchman didn't come after us. From that distance, I'm sure he couldn't tell if we were boys or girls. If he thought we were boys, maybe he just didn't want to be bothered with the hassle of chasing us. Or maybe he just viewed it as three kids, out after hours, engaging in a bit of harmless fun. We weren't bothering anybody. We weren't destroying or vandalizing the State's property. We weren't making out with the opposite sex. We never found out why he didn't come after us. We were just happy that he didn't.

When we went out to play that afternoon, the girls in our cottage hid apples under their shirts so we could share them with our friends. Every so often, we would have to go inside to "use the bathroom" so we could sneak out more apples. We saved some for ourselves, but most of the apples were gone in a day. And Old Hawkear never knew.

I pretty much avoided Miss B and she ignored me, until the day she lost her mind on me. When I was in Taft, Betty ironed my clothes. When I was in Peter Pan, Miss Mildred helped the supervisors with the ironing. In Garfield, I had to iron my own clothes. I was only ten years old and had never ironed before, and wasn't sure how high to set the iron. I set it too high and I burned the sleeve of my favorite blouse, one that Daddy bought for me. I rinsed it in cold water and hung it on the line in the basement. When Miss B saw the blouse, she got mad. She sent for me to come downstairs. As I reached the landing, she started yelling at me. She said I was a good-for-nothing black brat, and that I deliberately burned my blouse.

"Why would I deliberately burn my favorite blouse?"

"Because you're too lazy to iron it," she answered.

"If I was going to burn something on purpose, it wouldn't be the blouse Daddy gave me."

"I'm not going to argue with you," she said. "I told Miss Ferguson this wouldn't work. You people need to stick with your own kind. I didn't want you stinking niggers in my cottage anyway."

I started down the steps toward her. "What did you say?"

She turned red and started screaming at me. "Don't you come near me! You get away from me!" She ran toward her office, with me hot on her heels. As I neared the doorway, she reached for her paddle and held it high over her head. "Stay away from me!"

"You're not going to hit me with that thing."

"I'll break it over you head if you take one more step. Get out of here, you black nigger." By this time, most of the girls in the cottage were in the hall, yelling and screaming at her. She started to swing the paddle at me. I grabbed it and we tussled over it. I ended up with it in my hand. She ran into her bedroom and locked the door. I sat at her desk, holding the paddle, waiting for her to come out.

Dean was in Garfield B. I don't know who told her, but I could hear her yelling through the adjoining door. Miss Hamilton, her supervisor, was blocking the doorway so Dean couldn't come over to my cottage.

Pam Streeter ran out the back door to get Roxanne, who had just left dining room detail. Roxanne came to the office and asked me what happened. After I told her, she said, "Gibby, give me the paddle."

"No. She said she was going to break it over my head. When she comes out, that's exactly what I'm going to do to her."

"No you're not. Give it to me."

"I thought you'd be on my side. She called me a black brat and a stinking, black nigger. How can you take her side over mine?"

"I'm not taking sides. But you can't go around hitting adults with paddles. Now give it to me."

I was so disappointed in her. I shoved the paddle in Roxanne's hand and stormed into the living room. She told Miss B it was safe to come out. Miss B cracked the door. When she was certain that I was gone, she came out and sat at her desk. "I don't know what happened to her. She just went crazy. I told Miss Ferguson this would never work. I'm not the only one who said so either."

Roxanne just sat on the couch and listened to her go on and on. Finally Roxanne said, "Miss B, did you call her a black brat? Did you call her a nigger?"

"Well, yes, I did. That's what she is. That's what they all are."

Roxanne stood, very slowly and deliberately. She spoke in a very quiet monotone. "Don't you ever call her that again. If you do, you won't have to worry about a skinny little ten-year old coming after you. I will take this paddle and shove it so far up your big butt that you'll have splinters in your ears. And if you think I'm playing with you, try me. Go ahead. Call her a nigger now. You think you hot stuff messing with that skinny little girl. Well, if you're so tough, try messing with me."

"Roxanne Duncan, you can't talk to me like that. I'll. . ."

Before she finished, Roxanne cut her off. By this time, Roxanne was shouting. "You're not going to do anything! And you can't call her names like that. They don't like this integration stuff any more than you do. But at least they're trying. And you? You're just a prejudiced fat pig."

Roxanne threw the paddle on the floor and said, "And you might as well put that thing away. You won't be using it on anybody," and she left the office. As she started down the hall, Cricket said, "She's in the living room."

I was sitting at the table, boiling mad. Pam sat on one side, and Crystal Allen was on the other. I don't remember who sat across from me. Most of the girls in the cottage were in there. As Roxanne walked in, they stepped back so she would have a clear path to me.

She put her hand on my shoulder and said, "Come on, Gibby, let's go upstairs." I stood and Roxanne put her arm around my waist. We walked up the stairs. Although I'm sure she wanted to many times, Miss B never called Marci or me a nigger again.

# Chapter 11

ॐ

We hadn't had a full Christmas vacation since we'd been in the Home. We usually went home for a day or two. But this year, we were going for the full week. I was really excited about that. I didn't have a clue what I'd do when I got home. I didn't know if Daddy had something planned or not, and it didn't matter. I'd be away from the Home for a week. And we'd get to see Lewis.

We hadn't seen him in about two years. He had come up to the Home with Daddy a few times. The last time, just before he was sent to Germany, he wore his Army uniform, and the girls just about went crazy. Lewis was so tall and so very handsome, with smooth, chocolate brown skin. The whites of his eyes were so white and clear and he had the most beautiful smile. He had carried me from the Den to the cottage on his shoulders. Cinderella, riding in her carriage to the ball couldn't have felt any more special than I did riding on Lewis' shoulders that day.

Christmas morning, Miss Bailey, one of the social workers, came to the cottage to tell me that there had been a change in plans. I didn't need to take my suitcase because

I'd be coming back to the Home that night. She wouldn't say anything else. I don't remember how we got home that day or who brought us back.

We filed into the house. As always, Daddy had the tree up, filled with decorations. Packages were strewn all over the floor. Christmas cards adorned the doorway between the front room and the middle room. It looked like Christmas, but something was wrong. It didn't feel like Christmas.

Daddy was sitting on the couch, looking very somber. We walked over, one at a time and kissed him. "Merry Christmas, Daddy" we said. He reached up and patted a back or touched a cheek, but he didn't say anything. Ben was the last one to come in. When he looked up and saw Ben, Daddy burst into tears. Ben hugged him and said, "It's all right, Daddy. It's all right." Ben motioned for Ed, who had sat beside Daddy, to move. He sat in Ed's place and put his arm around Daddy's shoulders. After a few minutes, Daddy spoke.

"Well, we got our Christmas present this morning."

We were excited. "What is it, Daddy?" "Where is it?" We all wanted to know.

He paused and let out a deep sigh. He didn't know how to say it. How does one couch such news, and on Christmas day at that? He just blurted it out.

"Ike's dead."

Betty screamed and clutched at her throat. Her necklace broke. White beads flew all over the room. She got up and ran out of the room, with Dean following close behind. Buster took my hand and we began to cry. Ben collapsed into Daddy's arms and shouted, "No! No! No!" over and over again. Bob and Ed sat very still with tears streaming down their faces. Nobody spoke or asked any questions. Ben got up and went outside. He stood out in the front yard, near the gate, in the snow, staring off into space, crying. A short time later, Bill arrived. I don't remember who told him or how he reacted.

I just sat there, unable to move. *This isn't happening. Lewis can't be dead. He was only twenty years old. Oh God, how could this happen? How could you let Lewis die? And on Christmas morning? That isn't fair. Every time I think of Christmas, I'll think of Lewis, dead, and Daddy crying, and my sisters screaming.* Suddenly, I didn't like Christmas anymore.

I don't remember what Daddy said about how Lewis died; only that someone shot him. Later, I heard two different stories about the circumstances surrounding the shooting. Neither story mattered. I knew that my big brother, my hero, was dead. It didn't matter who shot him or why. He was dead and I'd never see him again.

We went back to the Home that evening. By the time we got back, everybody knew what had happened. In typical Orphan fashion, my friends did little things to make me feel better. My bed was covered with love tokens; a candy cane, home-made cards, letters, an orange, and some ribbon candy. I sat on my bed and started reading the notes when the girls began to file in, one or two at a time. Nobody knew what to say. We just sat on my bed in silence until we dozed off.

The day before the funeral, we were in the dining room for dinner. Emma, who was still in Taylor B, came over to our table and said something to Mrs. Vincent. Mrs. Vincent nodded and Emma came over to me. She told me Miss Allen wanted to see me. I went with Emma to her table. Miss Allen had tears in her eyes. She hugged me and said, "I know you loved your brother very much. I am so sorry for your loss, but we just have to trust and believe in God." Then she handed me an envelope. I thanked her and went back to my table. I didn't open the envelope until I returned to the cottage. It was a sympathy card, a beautiful card. I didn't remember anyone at the Home ever doing anything like that before. Miss Ferguson, the Dean of Girls on the main campus, always gave us birthday cards, but they were recycled. She would collect cards from the Women's Auxiliary and from other adults, cut off the signature, and sign them "Love, HF", and stuff them in brown, number ten envelopes. Most of the time, the cards didn't even fit in the envelopes. But this was a new card, one that was bought especially for me.

I'd always had mixed feelings about Miss Allen. Sometimes I loved her and believed that she loved me. Other times, I hated her and knew that she hated me. But at that moment, everything she had ever done to me and to the other girls seemed less important than that one act of genuine kindness. And I loved her for that.

We left for the funeral the next day. By the time we got to the house, Miss Jenkins, the minister, and the funeral directors were already there. We stood in the living room and prayed, then piled into the cars for the service. I don't remember much about the service, who said what or who sang what. I remember Ben grabbing on to the casket and falling to the floor. Daddy and some man had to pry his hands loose and help him back to his seat. He just kept saying, "Ike! Ike!" Daddy and Ben were the only ones who called him that. He was named Isaac, like Daddy. The rest of us called him by his middle name, Lewis.

Betty and Dean were wailing and moaning. And Daddy just looked so sad, like he did when he sat in that red chair at Miss Jenkins' house when Mama died.

After the service, we sat in the limousine as the flowers were loaded into the hearse. We had all calmed down a bit by this time. A man and a little boy came over to the car. The man whispered something to the little boy, who was about four years old. The boy climbed up on Daddy's lap, hugged Daddy, and said, "Mr. Gibson, I'm sorry your son died."

Daddy hugged him for a long time. I kept looking at that little boy. It seemed as if I should know him. Daddy put him down, and thanked him and his father for coming. As they

walked away, Daddy turned to us and said, "That was Tiny."
I completely lost control. I wanted to go after them. I was
sitting on Ben's lap and he wouldn't let me go. I wanted to
grab that little boy and hug him. I wanted to tell him, *The
man in that casket is not just my father's son. That man is
your big brother and I am your big sister. And all those other
kids in the car are your brothers and sisters. And that old
man, the one whose lap you just sat on, is your father.* Why
didn't anybody tell him? Why didn't Daddy tell him? Was I
the only person who believed he had a right to know?

That was the first time I had seen Daved since he had been
adopted. I wouldn't see him again until he was twenty-one
years old.

I was pretty much in a daze for the rest of the year. If anything eventful happened, I don't remember it. This was a little different from when Mama died. Though I loved her
dearly, I really didn't know her. Besides, she was old; forty-
two seemed old to me. You expect old people to die. But
Lewis was only 20, and he was my big brother. He wasn't
suppose to die. He was too young. On the outside, I seemed
normal. But on the inside, I was dying.

$$\Diamond$$

I dreaded the upcoming graduation. Ben would be leaving. I didn't want to deal with that. Graduations were always
hard on us, all of us. Even if we didn't know anyone graduating, we cried. The relationships we had with each other
were the most important things in our lives. We became
family. Some of us didn't have any other family. There was
very little we wouldn't do for each other. We lied to protect
each other. Sometimes, the stronger ones would accept punishment to protect the weaker ones. And to most of us, race
didn't matter.

On the girls' side, tears were like a flu epidemic; if one of
us cried, someone else did, and eventually, all of us would
end up crying. We viewed graduations as we did funerals, an

end, rather than a beginning. Even though the graduates distributed inscribed pictures that said, "I'll see you soon" or "I promise to stay in touch", they seldom did. And if they did, they didn't do so for long.

The week prior to graduation was filled with activities, the senior band concert; senior strings recitals, senior choir concert, Baccalaureate, then graduation.

Betty and Dean took it really hard. We couldn't believe Ben was really leaving. He and I didn't interact much. I'd see him in the dining room, the auditorium, and in church and that was about it. Sometimes, I'd run into him on the way to school. We could talk for a few minutes then. But most of the time, we didn't even have a chance to chat. And now, he was leaving. I didn't think I'd ever get to talk with him again.

I had just lost Lewis, and now I was losing Ben too. I didn't want to go to the graduation, but I didn't have any choice. As soon as we entered the auditorium, I started crying. I didn't stop until long after I was in bed that night. Betty would leave in two years. That night, I began to prepare myself for that day.

All kinds of groups and organizations came to the Home to visit with us or to take us off campus for a few hours. I rarely got to go with them. But during the summer of 1961, a Brownie Scout Troop from Yellow Springs wanted to take some of us on a picnic at John Bryan State Park. The Troop had two eleven-year old colored girls. Marci and Bootsie were the only other colored girls in the Home who were my age, but they were on vacation with their mother at the time. So I was selected, along with about ten other girls, to go to the park with the Brownies.

The two colored girls were named Marsha Ross and Tanya McDonald. We hit it off right away. We played and sang and laughed and talked. We had a ball. When it was time for us to go back to the Home, we exchanged addresses and promised to write to each other. I didn't believe they'd write to me, and I didn't want to write first. I'd be devastated if they didn't answer.

After lunch one day, Miss B called me into her office. "Who do you know named McDonald who lives in Yellow Springs?"

"Some girl I met when we went to John Bryan with the Brownies. Why?"

She thrust a brown, 6 x 9-inch envelope at me. "Here. You have some mail."

I ran upstairs to my room. I sat on the bed and nervously opened the envelope. Inside was an autograph book made of different colored construction paper. It was hole punched and tied together with yellow yarn. Tanya had signed the first page and included a school picture. In her letter, she told me how much fun she'd had with me. She said she told her parents and her sisters and brother all about me and she wanted to know what they had to do to come visit me. I wanted to scream. I was so excited. I grabbed a tablet and immediately wrote a letter to her.

We wrote to each other for several weeks. Then one Sunday, Miss B called me downstairs during rest period. As I neared the top of the steps, she said, "You have company."

I ran downstairs, expecting to see Daddy or Miss Jenkins. When I walked into the living room, there stood Tanya, her mother and father, both of her sisters and her brother. I was so shocked. Tanya had said they'd come and visit. And as much as I wanted to believe her, I really didn't believe they would. Her mother came over and put her arm around me. "You must be Nancy. It's good to finally meet you."

I couldn't believe they really came. I was so touched that my eyes brimmed with tears. Mrs. McDonald patted my cheek and said, "My goodness, you really are a sensitive little thing, aren't you?"

We visited for almost two hours and they had to leave. Tanya said, "Do you want us come visit you again?"

"Yea. Will you?"

She looked at her parents. Her father said, "I think I can arrange that."

When they left, I went to my room and wrote Tanya another letter. I wrote to Marsha too. Marsha and I had written a few letters, but our friendship didn't click like Tanya's and mine did. I mailed the letters the next day. About one week later, Miss B called me to her office again. She was holding a package in her hands. It was wrapped in brown paper, and the words "Handle with Care" and "Fragile" were printed in large letters with a black marker. She said, "You have some mail from that McDonald girl. This thing is heavy as lead." As I reached for it, she dropped it on the floor. I could hear it breaking.

I yelled at her. "You did that on purpose, you hateful witch. I can't stand you." I picked the package off the floor and took it to my room. I peeled the paper off and tried to put it back together so I could see what it was. It was a Plaster of Paris plaque Tanya made for me. In the upper left hand corner and the bottom right hand corner she had painted the face of a colored girl. In the middle she had painted, "Nancy and Tanya. Friends Forever." She had painted a border of red, blue, and yellow flowers. I tried to glue it back together, but I couldn't. It was ruined. I wrote to Tanya and thanked her, but I had to tell her the truth. I had thrown it away because Miss B broke it.

I felt better when I got her next letter. In it she wrote, "Your supervisor can break a stupid ole plaque, but she can't break our friendship." We wrote to each other for a long time. We wrote about school and our friends and what we wanted to be when we grew up. And we made a pact that some day, when we were grown, I would name my first daughter Tanya Jean after her, and she would name her first daughter Nancy Jean after me. The McDonalds continued to visit for a few months, then the visits stopped. I was certain that I'd never see them again. Tanya and I continued to write for several years, though less frequently. Eventually, we stopped writing altogether.

◇

Other than an occasional tussle with my sisters, I hadn't been in any fights until the fifth grade. That year, I was in two. The first one was with Crystal Allen and Jenny Kooglar. I don't even remember what it was about. I just know that Crystal and I were fighting, when Jenny got involved. I ended up with a black eye. Crystal had a busted lip.

The other fight was with Dina Potter. She had been in the Home about three weeks, and she wasn't the friendliest kid around. She had an older sister and several brothers who came to the Home before she did. We never knew why she didn't come with the rest of them.

We tried to befriend her, but she just ignored us. If we tried to initiate a conversation, she wouldn't even look at us, much less answer us. We were at the pool one day. Jenny Kooglar said something that Dina didn't like. They tussled in the water for a few minutes when someone broke them up. It was over. So we thought. We were trying to get a group together to play water polo, and were standing by the side of the pool. Dina swam over to that side of the pool. As she got out, she deliberately kicked Jenny in the back of the head and ran to sit with the lifeguard.

When we got back to the cottage, we demanded to know why she kicked Jenny. She wouldn't answer. I said, "I know you're the newkie, but even a newkie should know that you can't go around kicking people." She still didn't say anything. I said, "What's wrong with you? All we've ever done was try to be your friends. Do you think you're better than we are?"

She said, "Did I ask you to be my friends? I have my own

friends. I don't want to be friend with any of you, especially not an ugly, black nigger."

I hit her hard. She tumbled backward through the doorway. The fight was on. We ended up at the top of the steps. Girls were crying and running out of the cottage yelling, "Fight! Fight! Dina Potter called Nancy Gibson a nigger and they're fighting."

Miss Samuels was the relief supervisor. She came upstairs with a paddle and tried to break us up. I told her to move before she got hurt. She left to get Miss Ferguson. Girls from other cottages were milling around our back door. When Josie, Dina's big sister, heard what was happening, she ran to our cottage. "Let me in." she demanded. Cecilia Clark stood in the doorway to block Josie from entering. "Let me in. She's fighting my little sister. Get out of my way."

Seemingly out of nowhere, Peggy Galvin stepped up and said, "Your little sister is three years older and at least twenty-five pounds heavier than Gibby. If she can't fight, then maybe she should keep her big mouth shut."

"You stay out of this, Peggy Galvin. You don't have anything to do with this." She turned back to Cecilia. "You let me in or I'll kick your butt."

Peggy pushed Cecilia out of the way, and stood in the doorway, toe-to-toe, nose-to-nose with Josie. "The only way you're going in this cottage is to kick my butt, and I don't think you can do that."

Josie backed down and ran to her cottage with tears streaming down her face. Not many girls would tangle with Peggy. Josie was a 'pretty girl,' about 5'8", maybe one hundred forty pounds. Peggy was only 5'4", about one hundred seventy-five pounds, and was built like a line backer. And she wasn't fat, just big, solid big, and she was strong and athletic. We didn't know if Peggy could really fight, but from the looks of her, we didn't want to find out.

Miss Ferguson came to the cottage and met with Dina and

Miss Samuels. Then she met with me in the living room. "I know it hurts when someone calls you that. It hurts me."

I wanted to say, *No, it doesn't hurt in the least. But as a colored child, I'm suppose to hit anybody who calls me a nigger.* But I just listened to her as she feigned concern and pain.

"But you can't go around fighting every time someone calls you a name."

*How well I know that! If that were true, I'd have beaten the living daylights out of Miss Allen and Miss Miller!*

She continued, "I've put Dina on punishment, but since you hit her first, even though you were provoked, I'm going to have to punish you too. You will have two weeks of fatigue. But you can work in my office. How about that?"

I guess that was suppose to make it all better! I said, "That's fine, Miss Ferguson."

When the girls told me what Peggy had done, I was surprised. After dinner, I went to her and thanked her. "Oh, it's o.k." she said. I heard you kicked Dina's butt."

"Well, I don't know about that."

Sarah Cummings, Peggy's cousin, and Bones Nielsen were sitting with her. Sarah said, "Do you think she'll wanna' fight you again?"

"Nah, I don't think so."

Peggy replied, "Well, then, you kicked her butt! Wanna' play four-square?"

"Sure." We headed for the court while Bones ran to get a ball from the equipment bag. I felt bad for Dina. I didn't like to fight. Being called a nigger didn't really bother me because I knew I wasn't a nigger. I guess there were just too may wrongs that day: wrong person in the wrong place at the wrong time saying the wrong thing. Dina was on the receiving end of a lot of frustration and anger that were not really all hers. Yet at the same time, I felt pretty good for myself. I knew I could defend myself if I had to. It was especially good to know that I could do so against an older, heavier, seemingly stronger opponent. I didn't think I'd have to fight anyone again. And to top it all off, Peggy Galvin was my new friend.

# Chapter 12

❧

By the time we started sixth grade, a lot of my class-mates were on the main campus in Jefferson, though a few of them were still in Taylor. By now, Marci and I were roommates. Roxanne had run away several times. Her mother finally came and took her home. We all were sad to see her leave, but it was especially bad for Cricket. She spent more time with Roxanne than she did with her own sister. Roxanne said she'd keep in touch with us, but she didn't.

My sixth grade teacher was Mrs. Black. I loved being in her class. We had in-class spelling bees and played QuizMo. She talked a lot about her family, especially her children, Janice, Kenneth and Evelyn. Kenneth had polio as a child and walked on crutches. Betty had been in her class too. They liked each other a lot. As a baby, Betty had polio and had to wear a brace. She walked with a slight limp. I think Mrs. Black thought we shared a common bond—someone we loved had suffered with polio. I don't think she realized that I wasn't even born when Betty had it. It didn't matter though, because, for whatever reason, she liked me.

She made learning so much fun. We read and memorized

a lot of poetry. It was in her class that I started writing poetry. She submitted one of my poems for publication in our monthly magazine, The Home Review. It was rare for a sixth grader to be published in The Home Review, but I was. I started writing short stories too, but the Review didn't publish those. I just kept them in my dresser drawer with my poems.

Near the middle of the third quarter, a new family named Fitzgerald arrived. They were white and from "the hills of Kentucky." Howard, the second oldest, was in our class. They hadn't been in school much, so Howard was behind us in everything, especially reading. Mrs. Black told us about him before he arrived. "Now this young man has not been in school. He hasn't had the same privileges you have had. We will not tease him. We will not make fun of him. We will help him in any way we can, won't we boys and girls?"

"Yes, Mrs. Black," we all replied.

When Howard arrived, we were shocked to learn how far behind he was. He was reading from Dick and Jane. Sometimes, we'd take a short break in class and Mrs. Black would play music. She usually asked for a volunteer to sit with Howard to help him prepare for the spelling bee. It got to the point that we would almost argue over who would help him.

On the day of the spelling bee, Howard stood on one side of the room and about six of us lined up on the other. He wasn't given the same words we were. He was given words like "cat, the, we, and him." If Howard got a word that seemed to worry him, someone would whisper, "Take your time, Howard. You can do it." And he usually did. He had a total of twenty words to spell. And he spelled them all. We stood and clapped for him. I think it was all a bit over-whelming for him. As Mrs. Black draped a First-Place Medal around his neck, he began to cry. He thanked us for helping him and for not making fun of him. "At my last school, they teased me because I was stupid. You guys make me feel smart."

Of course, some of us started crying too. Becky Warren said, "But you're not stupid, Howard. You are smart. Look how much you learned in just a few weeks."

Mrs. Black told Howard to take his seat. She said, "We're going to take a restroom break now, and when we return, since it's such a nice, sunny day, we'll continue our lessons outside."

We almost broke our necks getting to the bathroom and back. It wasn't often that the elementary school had lessons outside. Sometimes, we'd look out the window and see the high school kids sitting on the ground under shade trees or in the sun, doing their lessons. We couldn't wait until we were in high school so we could study outside.

Mrs. Black got some cookies from her storage closet and we went outside and sat under a large maple tree. She was so proud of us. I wasn't really sure why. What we did for Howard, we would have done for anyone. We were Orphans, and we stuck together. Didn't she understand that? Though we certainly appreciated it, she didn't have to reward us for that.

I had been taking piano lessons for a year. Jean Blackwell, Kimberlyn Travis, and I shared a forty-five minute lesson. Kimberlyn, being a nearly straight-A student, always went first. Jean practiced second, and I was last. They were both in the seventh grade and had a full year of lessons when I started. Naturally, I wasn't as good as they were.

I seldom got my full fifteen minutes. Whatever time was left after Mr. Cooke worked with Kimberlyn and Jean, was all the time I got. Sometimes, I got ten minutes; sometimes I got five minutes. After hearing the same thing over and over, I knew how to play it. It wasn't until the end of the first quarter that he discovered I couldn't read a note.

I didn't care for Mr. Cooke. He was too fresh. We had heard a lot of stories about him. He would rub the girls' backs to see if they wore bras. If they did, his hand would 'accidentally' slip from their shoulders and down the front of their blouses. And if we didn't wear bras, he would look to see if we needed to. If so, we got the 'accidental' hand slip too.

I had told the girls, on many occasions, that if Mr. Cooke touched me, I'd slap him. Well, came the day when I had to put up or shut up. I was sitting at the piano when Mr. Cooke's hand 'accidentally' slipped off my shoulder. He hadn't done the old 'search for the bra strap test'. He didn't need to. He could see that I needed a bra. I 'accidentally' got up and backhanded him. "Don't you touch me like that, you dirty old creep."

"Who do you think you are, girl?"

"It doesn't matter who I think I am. You can play touchy feely with these other girls all you want, but don't you dare touch me like that again."

"You sit down and practice your lesson."

"If you move away from the piano."

"Don't come into my class and tell me what to do. I'm the teacher. Now sit down and play your lesson."

"I won't. Not until you move. You ought to be ashamed, getting fresh with a bunch of kids."

"You little nappy-headed pickininny. Either you sit down and play your lesson, or go to the office."

I walked to the doorway and turned around for one last statement. Jean and Kimberlyn were sitting there with their mouths hanging open, eyes as big as frying pans. They couldn't believe I'd hit him. Neither could I.

"And you, Mr. Cooke, can go straight to hell, you dirty old man." As I walked out and slammed the door, he yelled, "Don't you ever come back to my classroom again."

I surprised myself. I had never cursed before. Then, I got scared. I had to go to the principal's office and explain why I was kicked out of piano class. *Man, am I going to get it now. I have to tell Mr. Williams that I had just hit a teacher and told him to go to hell.* I could see it now—a spanking, detention, cottage confinement, and who knew what else!

I told Mr. Williams what happened. "You slapped Mr. Cooke? Who do you think you are? You can't go around slapping teachers!"

"But Mr. Williams, he had no business putting his hand down my blouse."

"You're not the first one to try that, young lady. We've heard those rumors before and we don't believe them. Mr. Cooke is a respected teacher. He's been here for a long time. I doubt that he would deliberately do anything like that. If it happened, and I'm not saying that it did, but if it did, I'm sure it was an accident."

"It was about as accidental as me slapping him."

"Now you watch your mouth, young lady. Don't make matters worse by getting smart with me."

I knew it was useless to argue with him. He wasn't going to believe me. Why confuse him with truth when he already had an opinion? I just sat there while he lectured me. My punishment wasn't bad, though. I had to stay after school and clean the blackboards and erasers for a week. In addition to my regular homework, I had to write "I will not slap a teacher" 500 times. Fortunately, the next day, I had to give it to Mr. Williams and not to Mr. Cooke. And, of course, since I got in trouble at school, I got in trouble at the cottage too. I was put on detention again.

Mr. Williams hadn't been the principal for very long. He took over as principal when Mr. Waldron left. I liked Mr. Williams. His sister was the girls' gym teacher. He was a lot nicer than she was. He was nicer than most of the adults. And he seemed fair. We'd heard stories about different adults who were mean, and had been warned not to get on their bad side, but I don't remember hearing any horror stories about Mr. Williams. And I thought he was handsome. I didn't put him in the same league as Harry Belafonte, Yul Brenner, and Gregory Peck, but he was a nice-looking man.

By the time school was out that day, everybody knew what happened in piano. Jean and Kimberlyn had told their friends, who told their friends, and soon, it was all over the campus. Nobody could believe that I actually slapped Mr. Cooke. But they didn't really understand what happened. Several girls had complained about Mr. Cooke. Once, in front of about ten witnesses, I said that if he touched me, I'd slap him. We had a long conversation about that and nobody believed I'd do it. Well, he touched me, in front of two witnesses. I had to hit him. Yes, I was angry that he touched me, but it wasn't so much about indignation as it was about saving face in front of the other girls. I had to prove that my word meant something. And I did. I was good at piano, and really wanted to stick with it. But that was now beyond my control. I never took another piano lesson.

◇

Rachel came to the Home that year, along with her brother Rob, who was in my class, and her sister Pam. Her brother George was already there. I never knew why they didn't all come at the same time.

Rachel was the cutest little girl, and the first red-haired, freckle-faced colored child I had ever seen. I liked her immediately. She was eight and I was twelve. I had always wanted a little sister. I was close to a couple of little white girls, but there was just something about Rachel that really touched me. We decided to adopt each other.

When I was about eight, Miss Jenkins bought me a sailor suit. It was a little big, but I wore it anyway. It was light gray, with red piping on the collar and on the sleeves. The jacket was double-breasted with four brass buttons and was lined in red satin. The skirt had big box pleats. That was my favorite outfit. I liked it better than my blue car coat.

At twelve, I was still a little thin, so I could still get in the suit, but the sleeves were too short and so was the skirt. I wanted Rachel to have it. Back home, when Betty outgrew something, it went to Dean. When Dean outgrew something, it came to me. So it was natural that I wanted my 'little sister' to have my suit. I hung an old dress over it and put it in the back of the closet to hide it from Miss B until I could figure out how to get it to Rachel.

Just about every month, Miss B's daughter and granddaughter would come visit her on a Sunday afternoon. One Sunday, Jenny Kooglar came into my room. She said, "Gibby, you'll never believe it. Miss B's granddaughter is downstairs and she has on a sailor suit just like yours."

I went downstairs to see for myself, and sure enough, there she was in a light gray sailor suit. I had a strange feeling in the pit of my stomach. I ran upstairs and rifled through my closet. When I saw the old dress in the back, I felt a little better. It was still hanging where I had left it, in the very back of the closet against the wall. I took it out anyway, just to look at Rachel's suit. I took the dress off the hanger, but there was nothing under it. That child had on Rachel's suit! I was furious.

I marched back downstairs and right into Miss B's office. I looked at the child and said, "Nice suit. Where'd you get it?"

Miss B tried to tell her not to answer me, but it was too late. The child said, "Grandma."

I look at Miss B. "Is that my suit? Did you steal my suit out of my closet and give it to her?"

Miss B just looked at me. "Nobody invited you in here. Go back to your room."

"Is that my suit?" I wouldn't budge.

She said it again. "Get out of here and go to your room."

Her daughter and granddaughter were stunned. They just

stared at me. I looked at the little girl and said, "Your grand-mother says that I'm a filthy, stinking, black nigger. She avoids me because I guess she thinks it will rub off on her. You're wearing my suit. You better hope it doesn't rub off on you." I stormed back upstairs.

I was so mad. That was my suit. If she had wanted her granddaughter to have one, she could have bought one for her, or the child's parents could have bought one. It was mine, and I wanted to give it to Rachel. And if Rachel couldn't have it, it should have gone to another Orphan. That child had a lot of nice clothes and shoes and her parents had money; at least they looked like they did. Of all the mean, nasty things Miss B did, at the time I thought that was one of the worst.

# Chapter 13

That summer, I transferred to Monroe B. I roomed with Linda Streeter. Peter Boles was my seventh grade teacher. He had grown up in the Home, along with several of his siblings. He started teaching at the Home when I was in the fourth grade, and was the first colored teacher I had.

I had mixed feelings about him. By the time I reached the seventh grade, I'd heard a lot of rumors about how mean he was and how he sometimes got fresh with the girls. I didn't know whether or not to believe the stories.

We had two sets of brothers and sisters in our class, the Sweeneys and the Warrens. With both families, it seemed that the brothers had a harder time than their sisters did. Mr. Boles stayed on those boys all the time. He mercilessly teased them about being dumber than their sisters. Once, when Randy Warren forgot to do his homework, Mr. Boles had his sister, Becky, stand at the blackboard. He drew a circle on the board where her nose would touch, then told her to sit down. He called Randy up front and told him to put his nose in the circle. Randy was about two inches shorter than Becky. He had to stand on his toes with his nose in that circle for about ten minutes.

And Mr. Boles had hot alleys. I hated the hot alleys. Those of us who passed our spelling tests would form two lines facing each other. Those of us who failed had to walk between the two lines while the rest of us hit them with our rulers. If we didn't hit as hard as Mr. Boles thought we should, he would hit us with a yardstick. And it didn't matter where his yardstick fell – a shoulder, the back of the head, wherever. Sometimes, he would make us hit them again and again until he was satisfied that we had hit hard enough. Ted Sweeney failed a lot of spelling tests. And his sister, Lisa, had to hit him. Every time we had a hot alley, she cried, whether Ted had to go through or not.

Around Easter time, Mr. Boles did something that really surprised me. I had been pressing my own hair for some time. So had Bootsie. We didn't do a very good job, though. Mr. Boles asked permission to take us to a shop in town to have our hair done for Easter. Surprisingly, we were allowed to go. He picked us up on Saturday morning and dropped us off at Randy's, near Wilberforce University. Randy was suppose to be the best beautician in the area. And we didn't just go to Randy's shop; Randy himself did our hair. We had a ball, listening to the tales told by the customers and beauticians. I didn't know how much was truth and how much was fantasy, but the tales were dramatic and funny. Randy had music playing the whole time. Every so often, someone would shout, "Ooooh! That's my song!" and they'd start dancing. They taught us a few dances. My favorite was the Monkey.

Mr. Boles came back a few hours later to pick us up. On the way back, we stopped to get something to eat. He didn't seem so bad. I thought the rumors about him might not be true at all. At the very least, they may have been exaggerated.

In science class one day, he asked a question. No one raised a hand. He sat on his desk in the front of the class and started calling names, beginning at the front of the row where I sat. As he continued calling names in my row, some said, "I don't know." Others shrugged. Some neither said nor did anything. When he came to me, I shrugged my shoulders and said, "I don't know."

He jumped off the desk and ran down the aisle. He had the hard-bound textbook in his hand. When he got to my desk, he swung the book, catching the entire left side of my head and face. He hit me so hard I fell out of my seat and wet my pants. I was stunned for a few seconds. When I got up, he hit me again. He berated me and said I should be embarrassed for being so stupid. As he walked back to his desk, he said to the class, "Since you're on your way to art, maybe somebody should make a dunce cap for the chowder head in the back."

As the rest of the class left for art, he took me to the principal's office. Mr. Williams wasn't in so Mr. Boles proceeded to lecture me. He said, "You don't even know why I hit you, do you? You're too stupid to know what you did."

I responded, "I did what everybody else did. I said I didn't know."

He shrugged his shoulders two or three times and contorted his face. His movements and mannerisms were grossly exaggerated. "I don't know. I don't know. Don't you know what that looks like? Stepin Fetchit. That just what you looked like."

"What is Stepin Fetchit?" I asked.

"Stepin Fetchit is not a what. Stepin Fetchit is a who. See. You don't even know who he is!"

"If I've never seen him or heard of him, then how am I suppose to know who he is?"

He rose and glared at me. "I ought to hit you again."

I raised my chin slightly so he could have easy access to the right side of my face. The left side was already swollen. I could look down and tell that I had a big shiner. "Get out of my sight," he yelled. "You make me sick." I left and went to art.

He hit a lot of kids, but the only other girls in my class who were really beaten were Junie Bivins and Cissy Sanders. Like me, they ended up bruised and swollen. But they each received an apology and he had a conference with the principal about his disciplinary methods. He told Junie, "It doesn't take much of a man to beat a woman. I wasn't acting like much of a man today and I'm sorry. Please forgive me." He apologized to Cissy and asked her forgiveness too. Even their supervisors met with the Dean of Girls to complain about how he beat their girls.

That sent a very clear message to me. He never apologized to me. He wasn't summoned to the principal's office for a conference. Nobody met with Miss Ferguson to discuss their outrage about what he did to me. What that told me was that even as a teacher, there were boundary lines that he, as a colored man, could not cross when it came to the white girls. As for me, there were no boundaries. He could blacken my eyes, bloody my mouth, say whatever he wanted, never apologize, and nobody would say or do anything about it. As Orphans, we were treated as if we were a subspecies. As a colored Orphan, I was treated as if I were lower than that.

What a disappointment he was. I wasn't expecting to be the teacher's pet just because we were both colored. But I was expecting some level of connection. He was one of only three colored teachers the whole time I was in the Home, and the only colored teacher I had. Having grown up in the segregated Home himself, I assumed he would have understood my need to identify with someone who looked like me. I assumed we would have had a lot in common. I couldn't have been more wrong. Aside from being colored Orphans, we had nothing in common.

And he never did tell me who Stepin Fetchit was.

I was having problems in Monroe. We all had come to the conclusion that Mrs. Wagner was truly crazy. We thought most of the adults were, but her craziness was different. Most of them were consistent in their hatefulness and meanness. But Mrs. Wagner would love us one day, and despise us the next. And she didn't just single out one or two people. She was like that with all of us, except Candi Lawson. No matter what the situation or circumstance, Candi could do no wrong.

Every Wednesday, we had cottage inspection, so on Tuesday evenings before study hall, we had to clean our rooms. It was Linda's turn to mop our floor since I had done it on Saturday. When she finished, she asked me to take the bucket to the basement while she jumped in the tub. I took the bucket downstairs, emptied it, and sat with Peggy and Darla Potts until study hall started.

While we were doing our homework, Mrs. Wagner went upstairs to check our rooms. Candi's room was next to ours. She had left her bucket in the hall. Old Wagner immediately assumed it was ours. After completing her inspection, she came downstairs with the bucket in her hand. She slowly walked over and stood behind Linda, and threw the bucket at her. There were six girls sitting at the table, all of whom got wet. The bucket hit Linda in the back of the head. "You slop hog!" Wagner shouted. "You can't even bring a lousy bucket downstairs and empty it."

Linda started crying. I yelled from my table on the other side of the room. "That is not Linda's bucket!"

"You keep your big slop mouth out of this. This doesn't have anything to do with you."

"Yes it does. I brought Linda's bucket downstairs and emptied it. That bucket belongs to Candi."

"Candi wouldn't leave her bucket in the hall. Only a nasty slop hog would do something like that."

"Why don't you ask Candi?" She walked over to her chair and sat down. "Ask her. Since she's so perfect, I'm sure she wouldn't lie. Ask her if that's her bucket." She didn't respond. "Candi, is that your bucket?"

Wagner spoke. "Candi, you don't have to answer her. Don't you say a word."

Linda was sitting there soaking wet in thin, cotton pajamas, sobbing. Nearly everybody was crying. I was so angry I couldn't have cried if I had wanted to. I screamed at her. "You crazy old bat!"

She screamed back. "You shut your big slop mouth!"

"Make me! Come on. Make me!"

"Well, there's somebody in the main building who'd be happy to make you. She's been dying to get her hands on you for a long time."

"Go get her. I am not afraid of Miss Williams. Well, go on. Get her!"

I was so mad I was trembling. She got up and left the cottage. The girls were panic stricken. Several of them ran upstairs to peek out the windows. I told Linda to go change her pajamas. Bones told me to change my clothes too and run away. Most of the girls were afraid of Miss Williams. Whenever the supervisors had trouble with their girls, they would get Miss Williams. She'd come to the cottage, smack the girls around a bit, intimidate them into silence, and leave.

Darla came downstairs with about $1.25. "This is all the money I have. You can have it, but you have to go. Miss Williams will kill you."

"I'm not scared of Miss Williams."

Girls were running upstairs, getting whatever money they had, and bringing it to me. There was about eight dollars on the table. Peggy asked, "If Miss Williams hits you, will you hit her back?"

"I don't know. But I don't think she'll hit me."

Peggy finally admitted what we had known for months.

"Well, she beat the stuffing out of me. I'm a lot bigger than you are. If she wasn't afraid to beat me, why do you think she's afraid to beat you?"

"I don't think she's afraid to. I just don't think she will."

"Just take the money and go. Please."

"Look, I'm not going anywhere. If Miss Williams hits me, she just hits me. If I hit her back, then I hit her back. But I'm not going anywhere. I'm not afraid of her. Maybe I should be, but I'm not."

Bones whispered to Darla, "Man, she must be crazy. You'd have to be crazy not to be afraid of Miss Williams."

I turned to Bones and said, "Maybe I am. Maybe "crazy" is contagious. And if it is, I caught it here. I wasn't crazy until I came to this crazy place. You can't live in a nut house for long without going nuts!"

Old Wagner came back about twenty minutes later. She went straight to her room. There was a lot of whispering about whether or not Miss Williams was with her and if not, whether she was coming later. I still wasn't afraid. Around 8:30, we went upstairs to our rooms. Linda had a bump on the back of her head about the size of a small egg. She thanked me for taking up for her and apologized for getting me in trouble.

"How do you figure you got me in trouble?" I asked.

"Because, I saw Candi's bucket and I started to take it downstairs, but I didn't. I should have known Wagner would blame one of us. If I had just emptied Candi's bucket, none of this would have happened."

"The truth is, if Candi had emptied her own bucket, none of this would have happened. And it doesn't matter anyway, 'cause even if Candi had emptied her bucket, Old Wagner would have found something else to fuss about. She may not have fussed at you, but you can bet she would have fussed at someone."

As usual, we were in bed at 9:00. It wouldn't have been

unusual for Miss Williams to show up around 9:30 or so, summon me to Wagner's room, and rough me up; but she didn't. The next morning, it was business as usual. I expected Miss Williams to say something or do something when we had gym that week, but she didn't. I don't even know if Wagner really went to get her that night. For being so mouthy, I was confined to the cottage for a week.

◇

I was still in Monroe when I became aware of "gym parties". A lot of girls had been sneaking out after hours. Some were meeting with their boyfriends. Others were just roaming the campus, making their own fun. I don't know how long the adults knew that the girls were sneaking out, nor do I know how they determined who the girls were. Around 7:00 one evening, about sixteen girls were summoned to the square. They were told to form a line, single file, between Monroe and Hayes. They walked, on their knees, to the gym. Once there, they had to run, jump, exercise, and perform a variety of activities. The purpose was to expend all of their excess energy so they would be too tired to sneak out. At the end of the evening, each girl had to bend over and was whacked with a paddle that Miss Williams held like a baseball bat.

The next day, several of the girls were admitted to the hospital with knee infections. Denim fibers and bits of cement and dirt were imbedded in their knees. Three of the girls were from Monroe, including Rita McGregor. She had been in the Home about fourteen months. When she got out of the hospital, she called her mother.

A few days later when we were on our way back to the cottage after lunch, we noticed a car parked near the end of the sidewalk. Rita said, "That's my mom. I told you guys she was coming."

She broke ranks and ran to the car. Wagner yelled at her to come back, but she didn't. By the time we reached the cottage, Rita and her mother were walking up the sidewalk with two suitcases. Wagner started yelling. "What do you think you're doing?"

"I think I'm taking my daughter out of here."

"You can't do that!"

"I can and I will."

Old Wagner told Peggy to go get Miss Ferguson. Peggy turned and jogged, very slowly, toward Miss Ferguson's office. Wagner continued to yell. "You can't take her. She's state property. You'll be in jail."

"This is my child. I'll do what I want with her. Try to put me in jail if you want, but by the time you get to me, she'll be so far away from here you'll never find her." They ran into the cottage.

It took them less than fifteen minutes to throw Rita's belongings into the suitcases. They ran down the steps. Rita said, "If I left anything, you guys can have it. I love you guys. I wish I could take you with me. Gotta' go!"

Her mother was standing in the doorway. "Rita, come on!"

As Rita walked out of the door, she turned for one last comment. "Wagner, you're a crazy old battle axe. I hate your guts. I hope you rot in hell!" She ran to the car and yelled, "I love you guys. Don't forget me!"

We were so excited at the possibility that Rita would remain free. We felt as if we were in prison. Our only crime was being children born into families who, for whatever reason, couldn't take care of us. Watching Rita leave was like being in the middle of a James Cagney movie and all the convicts were cheering as he made his daring escape.

At the same time, we were afraid of what might happen to her and her mother. Rita was a ward of the State. Wagner said she could be charged with kidnapping. We didn't know if that was true; but if it was, we didn't want Rita's mother to go to prison. We understood prison life all too well.

We knew we'd miss Rita. She hated the Home and had

said, on many occasions, that when she got out, she'd never look back. We knew we'd never hear from her or see her again.

◇

In 1963, Betty and Dean left the Home. Betty graduated. Like a lot of Orphans, Dean needed another year to finish school. She could have applied for an extra year, but she didn't. She hated the Home too and was anxious to leave.

It was hard when Ben graduated, but it was harder when my sisters left. Though we all traveled in different circles, I found comfort in knowing that they were around if I needed them. Sometimes I felt secure just seeing them in the around campus.

Miss Jenkins and Daddy came to Betty's graduation. I wanted to beg them to take me too, but I didn't. I was still waiting for Miss Jenkins to take me on that weekend trip she had promised three years earlier. She or Daddy would get us for a week during the summer, and I usually went with the boys. Sometimes they'd get us all at Christmas. I just wanted a weekend by myself. I wrote and asked her if she could take me, just me, for a weekend. She wrote back and said, "The next weekend I'm off, I'll come and get you." But she never did. And I never reminded her. I was ten when I wrote that letter. I never asked her for anything ever again.

I didn't ask Daddy to take me because I had come to believe that if he had really wanted us, he would never have given us away in the first place. Besides, if he didn't come get me when he found about the beatings, I figured he wouldn't come get me because I was lonely.

And, of course, there was Ann, his wife. I was still upset with Daddy about that. It might have been easier if we had gotten to know her. But he showed up one Sunday with this woman we'd never seen or heard of and said, "This is my wife." I thought that was pretty cold. Besides, if he had wanted to take me, I'm not sure I could have lived with Ann, not in Mama's house.

I cried for two days after Betty and Dean left. After that, Daddy seldom visited. Neither did Miss Jenkins. Within a matter of months, neither of them visited at all.

◇

Not long after that, I was transferred to Taft A. Mrs. Wagner and I weren't getting along. That was no big surprise. She didn't get along with anyone for very long. Mrs. Buchanan was the supervisor. She reminded me of Miss Reutger. They were about the same age and size, had a similar hairstyle, and wore similar glasses. And like most of the supervisors, she was sometimey; sometimes nice, sometimes unpredictable. We didn't have too many problems though. We basically avoided each other.

She was off for a few days and Mrs. Clifford was the relief supervisor. We were in the living room one Saturday, waiting to go to the movie. The boys came over for their dates and she sent them away. We thought that was odd since she had already approved their date slips. About ten minutes later, we lined up at the door. We stood in line for about five minutes when Susie Hamilton went to tell her that it was time to leave for the auditorium.

She responded, "You won't be going to the movie tonight. In fact, just take off your clothes and go to bed."

We were livid. It was 7:20. We didn't have to be in bed until 9:00. Susie yelled at her. "Why? What did we do?"

"You know what you did. Now go to bed."

We just stood there looking at each other. No, we didn't know what we had done. Some of the girls started crying and went to their rooms. About half of us went into the living room. We were mad and we were not going to bed. We were thirteen and fourteen years old. We were not going to bed at 7:30. The kids in Peter Pan could stay up until 8:00 on Saturdays.

Mrs. Clifford came into the living room. "I don't know

what you girls think you're doing, but you'd better get to bed and I mean right now."

"Make us!" Susie Hamilton shouted.

She sat in the chair by the door. We just sat and glared at her. "Don't stop talking on my account," she said. "You had so much to say. Why don't you say it in front of me?"

After about fifteen minutes of bantering back and forth, she said, "Look, you know how things are done around here. If you don't like it, you can leave."

I finally spoke up. "Can we? I mean, if we head out that front door right now, will you try to stop us?"

She answered, "If you want to go, go. I won't do a thing."

I stood up. "All right. I'm leaving."

I started down the hall to change into some jeans. Susie, Samantha Hayes and Junie followed me. "Are you really going to leave?"

"I sure am. She said I could, so I am."

"Wait for me," Susie said. She went to her room to change clothes. Everybody took up a collection and by the time I was ready to go, six other girls joined me at the front door. We had almost $10.00. We said our goodbyes and walked out the door. As we crossed the parade field, we saw the night watchman. I spoke and waved to him. He waved and continued on his rounds. We had no idea where we were going or what we would do with $10.00. And we had no idea why the watchman didn't try to stop us, or at least question us.

We were almost to Cedarville when we stopped at a farmhouse. An old woman with white hair answered the door. We said we were part of a Girl Scout Troop on a night hike and asked her for something to drink. We waited on the porch as she came back with lemonade. As we sat on the porch, she asked a lot of questions. I was the spokesperson and answered most of them. We downed the lemonade, thanked her and I said, "Well, we're suppose to meet up with our Troop Leader in about fifteen minutes, so we'd better go." We didn't think for one minute that she believed us, so we left in a hurry. After she went back into the house and closed the door, we ran in the opposite direction, just in case she had called the police.

We came upon a little store that had bushels of apples sitting out front. We took some apples and went behind the store to rest and figure out what we were going to do. Samantha was crying because she was cold and had to go to the bathroom. "Go over there, behind those trees," I said. After she left, Susie and Junie said they wanted to leave her.

"She's a big crybaby," Junie said. "She's going to slow us down."

Samantha was a crybaby. She was bigger than all of us and had on more clothes than any of us. It was early October and though it was a little crisp, it wasn't really all that cold. But we couldn't leave her. As much as we wanted to, we knew we couldn't leave her.

When she came back, we got some more apples and tried to figure out where we would go. We lay on our backs, staring at the stars and talking about our dreams. Most of us had the same dream, living somewhere, anywhere, other than at the OS&SO Home. The houses we lived in, the things we did and the people we'd become were as different as we were, but all of us dreamed of a life outside of the Home.

For a brief moment, I thought about my life on Paisley Street when Mama and Daddy would make a pallet on the ground and we slept outside. That October sky was so dark and the stars were bright. We searched for the constellations, but the only ones I could ever find were the Big and Little Dippers.

About 15 minutes later, we saw flashing lights and heard two cars pull up in front of the store. Samantha had called the police from the pay phone in front of the store. They made us get in the cars and they took us back. We begged them to take us to jail instead, but they wouldn't. We spent the night in the hospital. Susie and Junie were placed in solitary confinement and the rest of us were spread out in different rooms. The next day, we went down to the cottage, all except Susie and Junie. They stayed in the hospital for two more days, though none of us knew why.

That was the first and only time I ran away. We had about four hours of freedom. We spent that time doing the same thing we always did, dreaming of a different life somewhere else.

A few months later, I was sent back to Monroe B. This time, I roomed with Peggy and her cousin, Sarah. They were the same age and I was a three years younger. We had a lot of fun together and were great roomies.

# Chapter 14

༉

I was very disappointed my first day in high school when I learned that Mr. Rooney would not be my English teacher. I had Mr. Bowers instead. I had waited for six years to be in his class. And on top of that, I was cut from his drama class. It was overbooked too. There were four freshmen in his class and we were all bumped out to the senior choir. I was also bumped from my vocational choice, working in the hospital. I had to take another year of typing and shorthand. I was good at both, but didn't like either.

By now, I was the only colored girl in my grade again. Bootsie left during the summer. Linda Franklin had come and gone within an eighteen-month period. It was just me again, and it would remain that way until I left.

Most of the girls in my class had boyfriends. Of the popular girls, I was the only one who didn't. Other than my brothers, there were about six colored boys of dating age, and every one of them, including my brothers, dated white girls.

Most of my teachers expected the worst from me, since I had a reputation of being a disturbed child and a troublemaker. I didn't think I was either. I just asked a lot of questions. I spoke up when I thought something was wrong. I knew that by speaking up, I would get in trouble. But sometimes, I just didn't care. Most of the time I didn't. I needed for them, all of the adults, to know that I knew they were wrong. Regardless of what they said, I wasn't state property. I wasn't anybody's property. And I wasn't about to let anybody treat me as if I were. The days of "Yassa' boss" and "Whatever you say, boss" had ended long before I was born. I was not about to resurrect them.

Other teachers tolerated me because I got good grades. But I got sick of them wanting me to be like Betty. Though everybody thought Betty and I looked alike and sounded alike, we were as different as night and day. Betty had the uncanny ability to accept things for what they were. If she thought the rules were stupid, she obeyed them anyway because they were the rules and because she was afraid to get in trouble. I, on the other hand, questioned what I thought was stupid. I needed to know why things were a certain way. I had a very difficult time accepting what I didn't understand, and trouble seemed to find me. Betty worked hard in school, appeared interested in school, and was a cheerleader. We both got good grades, but I didn't work very hard and showed very little interest in anything except drama, English, and eventually my hospital trade.

And unlike Betty and Dean, I had absolutely no interest in being a cheerleader. Poor Dean. Year after year, she tried out for cheerleader but she didn't make it. It didn't matter if she could jump higher or better than the other girls. And the fact that she ran away a couple of times shouldn't have mattered either. White girls who ran away more times than Dean made cheerleader. Although Dean wouldn't have been the first colored cheerleader, she certainly would have been the darkest. And that just wasn't how things were done at the OSSO Home. As I look back, I am reminded of an old song that says, "Fly in the buttermilk; shoo fly, shoo." Every year Dean tried to be the proverbial fly in the buttermilk. And every year she was told, "Shoo."

My first run-in with a high school teacher was with Mr. Brinson. He was a racist and everybody knew it. I shouldn't have been in his class anyway. Just like with piano, I was not in a class with my peers. I was the only 9$^{th}$ grader in his class with 11$^{th}$ grade algebra students. There were two or three 10$^{th}$ graders in there too. Every time I asked a question, he would either ignore me or tell me to quit acting stupid. One day he made a statement and asked, "Is that clear?" Nobody answered. He asked again. I said, "It's clear." He went berserk! He yelled at me and told me that I was a smart aleck. "Other teachers may take that stuff off of you, but I'm not having it in my class."

I was stunned. "What did I do?"

"You know what you did and I'm not having it. Now get out of my class."

I couldn't figure out what had just happened. Neither could anybody else. Charles Gaither spoke up. "Why are you yelling at her? What did she do?"

"You stay out of this. This has nothing to do with you. She knows what she did." He turned to me and said, "I want you out of here, now! Get out of my classroom. Get out!" His face was beet red and he was waving his arms and slamming things on his desk.

I was shocked and embarrassed, but I wasn't going to let him or anyone else know that. I laughed at him. "O.K.," I said. I gathered my books and papers and as I headed toward the door, I pointed at him and said, "And I'm the one they say is crazy?"

I never went back to his class. Instead, I spent forty-five minutes every day in the principal's office, teaching myself set theory, with occasional tutoring and tests from Mr. Williams. I didn't understand why they didn't just put me in the room with the rest of my class. But I didn't ask anybody about that. I knew that they would do exactly what they wanted, when they wanted, whether it made sense or not.

I was angry most of the time. Everything was going wrong. I didn't like my supervisor. I didn't like most of my teachers. I couldn't take the courses I wanted. Ninth grade was not turning out to be a very good year for me.

◇

My brother Bob had been dating a white girl named Mitzi. I was coming home from the dining room one day, when Lisa Beckman told me that Bob and Mitzi had been kicked out of the Home. I asked her why and she said she didn't know. I asked Mrs. Wagner if she knew anything about it. "That is none of your business," she said.

"He is my brother. How can you say that it's none of my business? I have a right to know."

"You don't have a right to know. You don't have any rights unless we say so. Now go to your room."

That evening, Rhonda Hathaway stopped me on the playground to tell me what happened. She said Mitzi was pregnant. I couldn't believe it. They actually had sex! We had suspected that some of the girls were having sex, but we didn't know for sure. Our minds had been so poisoned that we believed if a boy touched a girl's breast, she was a tramp and he was a sex maniac. Mitzi had been sent to an unwed mother's home in Columbus and Bob had gone to live with Daddy.

Ed was put out the same year. There had been a lot of problems in his cottage for a long time. Col. Garrison, the Dean of Boys, asked him to be a mediator of sorts. In the dining room one evening, Ed intervened in an on-going feud between Mick Stacey and Ozzie Mayfield. Mick and Ozzie were going to settle the feud after dinner. Ed said there would be no fighting. Mick and Ed exchanged a few words and the argument appeared to be over. When they left the dining room, Mick started in on Ed. He pushed Ed, so Ed hit him and knocked a tooth, a molar, right out of Mick's mouth. Ed was put out of the Home.

On the surface, it may have seemed appropriate, but when you consider that Charles Gaither broke Jeff Wallace's jaw a few months earlier, it seemed a bit harsh. Charles got detention and lost his ROTC rank. He was busted from Major to Private. By the time school started, Charles was the Major again. Both Ed and Charles were about to enter their senior year and neither of them had been in much trouble. None of us could understand why Ed was put out and Charles wasn't. Well, some of us understood. We just didn't want to admit it.

Nobody officially told me that Ed was leaving either. One day, he was just gone. I found out through my friends. I didn't get to say goodbye to Bob or Ed. Now just Buster and I were left.

Though a lot of girls in my class were still getting spankings and getting slapped, I wasn't. Miss Fredericks, the assistant dietitian, was the last person to hit me.

We were on detail, preparing for a banquet. I had already folded about a hundred napkins. Then I sat at a table for about half an hour, filling salts and pepper shakers. I put them on the tables. There was a group of about four or five girls sitting on the buffet, talking. They'd been there for fifteen minutes or so, doing nothing, while the rest of us worked. Since I hadn't had a break in well over an hour, I decided I would rest too. Miss Fredericks came out of the kitchen and told me to get busy.

"I'm taking a break."

"I didn't say you could take a break. You'll break when I say so."

"That's the problem. I've been working all along, and you haven't given me a break yet."

"Get up and get busy."

I pointed to the other girls sitting on the buffet. "What about them? Why don't they have to get busy?"

She was standing in front of me. "Because I didn't tell them to, that's why. I'm talking to you. Get up before I slap you."

I stood up. "You slap me, I'll slap you back."

She slapped me, hard. I slapped her back, just as hard. We left welts on each other's faces, but because she was white, hers were more visible than mine. She grabbed a tray from the buffet, and acted as if she were going to hit me with it.

"You hit me with that tray, and I'll ram it down your throat!"

Sgt. Gavin, the dietitian, came running over and stood between us. He told me to go to my cottage. Not many kids hit back, especially girls. In fact, I only remember two other girls who hit back the whole time I was in the Home. That was the kind of thing that would warrant getting Miss Williams to take care of. But it didn't happen. I was put on confinement again for two weeks.

In the tenth grade, I finally got to take drama and work in the hospital. I was so happy. I liked working in the hospital. Most of the kids didn't like Mrs. Neville. They thought she was mean, but I really liked her. She was strict, which is quite different from mean.

The kids didn't like Mrs. Blankenship much either. She was morbidly obese and overworked the kids. Doing some of the things she should have done exhausted her because of her weight. But she had a softer, nicer side to her too. And for some reason, they both seemed to like me. We had many conversations that had nothing to do with me being bad, keeping my grades up, or anything about the Home.

Sometimes, I was pulled from class to run blood tests and urine analysis on kids who suddenly spiked fevers. And, when it got really crazy in the cottage, I was sent to the hospital to work. Sometimes, if there was nothing for me to do, I just sat in the lab and read.

Celeste Simpkins came to the Home around this time. The OS&SO Home was not the place for her. She had seen her father kill her mother and had to testify at his trial. She had emotional problems that the Home was not equipped to handle. There were a few other children who had witnessed a parent's murder; in some cases, both parents. They should never have been in the Home either. And it didn't help that Celeste was nearly sixteen when she came to the Home. They usually didn't take kids that old.

Celeste was in my grade, but we didn't have any classes together. We became good friends. She was prone to "spells" of crying hysterically and no one could get her to say why except her closest friends. I was one of the few. And I, of course, wouldn't tell the adults what was wrong. We noticed that whenever she had a spell, they would send her to the hospital and she pretty much had her way. If she wanted me to come visit her, regardless of the hour, someone would send for me.

One day, we decided that we would use these spells to get what we wanted. I had vowed never to cry in front of them. But this was different. Now when I cried, it was because I chose to, not because of anything they had done to hurt me. They were masters of manipulation and control, and it didn't matter what methods they used to manipulate and control us. I saw how they reacted to Celeste when she had her spells. And it dawned on us how we could use those spells to manipulate and control them. When we wanted to create some excitement, a diversion from the humdrum boredom, we would cry.

We were in the dining room one night. Celeste turned, looked at me, and nodded her head. When she turned back around, we both placed our forks on our plates and began to cry. A few of the girls knew what was happening. The ones who didn't wanted to know what was wrong. Neither of us responded. Soon the other girls were crying too and Celeste and I really hammed it up. Our supervisors had someone escort us to the hospital. They were going to place us in separate rooms. We cried harder. Mrs. Blankenship was on duty and called Mrs. Neville at home. Mrs. Neville told her to give us valium and elevil and put us in the same room.

Mrs. Blankenship brought us a radio. The radio stayed in our room all night. We listened to music until we fell asleep. The next morning, they served scrambled eggs for breakfast. We wanted to see how far they would go, so we started to cry. We said we wanted fried eggs. We got fried eggs.

After the third or fourth time we were hospitalized for hysteria, we had to see the Home psychiatrist, Dr. Olsen. Neither of us talked to him much. We asked a lot of questions about what he would do with his reports. We didn't trust him. He was on the Home's payroll, so naturally anything we said to him would be repeated. He suggested that we both take valium and elevil on a regular basis. Celeste took hers, but I wouldn't. I pretended to, but I usually spit it out. Celeste got in more trouble because the medication made her sleepy and she would fall asleep in class. Since I wasn't sleeping in class, they assumed she was faking.

◇

Mrs. Harrigan was the new Dean of Girls. One evening after dinner, she sent for me to come to her office. When I arrived, she was sitting at her desk. She told me to sit in the waiting room for a few minutes. About five minutes later, Emma showed up. Mrs. Harrigan called both of us in. She said our supervisors had requested that we be removed from their cottages. "You two have been friends since, what, the first grade? But you haven't been in the same cottage since the Peter Pan. If I put you together, do you think you can behave?"

Emma reached over and took my hand. She squeezed it so hard I thought it would break. We tried not to smile or do anything to let her know how happy we were. I said, "We can try."

"All right," she said. "You will move to Taft B this weekend. Mrs. Vincent said she would take both of you. And you will be roommates."

We left her office holding hands and skipped all the way back to our cottages. Mrs. Vincent was really very decent to us. She just did what she was suppose to. She wasn't unusually mean or vicious, as some of the supervisors were. This is not a discovery I made as an adult looking back. I knew it then, which is why I cannot explain why I was determined to publicly humiliate her.

Everybody knew that, despite the dry rule, Mrs. Vincent was an alcoholic, and kept several bottles of wine in her room. One night, Julie, Cheryl, and Darlene created a distraction upstairs. When Mrs. Vincent went up to see what the commotion was all about, I went into her closet and took a bottle of Gibson's Wine, the only full bottle she had. I put the bottle in Hook Bolin's pillowcase and got in the shower. I was still in the shower when Mrs. Vincent came back downstairs. She went in her room and closed the door. A couple minutes later, she came out demanding that I come to her office. Hook told her I was in the shower. She said, "Get her. Tell her I want to see her now!"

Hook came to get me. I wrapped a towel around myself and went to her office. "You wanted to see me, Mrs. Vincent?"

Most of the girls were standing in the hall, right outside her door. "You took something that belongs to me and I want it."

"Me? I was in the shower. What's missing, Mrs. Vincent?"

"You know very well what's missing and I want it. Bring it here."

163

I continued to play dumb. "I don't know what you're talking about. Someone took something of yours and you think I did it? What did they take? What's missing?" I was determined to make her say it.

"A bottle of wine. Now bring it back."

"Ooooh! Mrs. Vincent, you know you're not suppose to have alcohol on campus. What if Mrs. Harrigan knew about this? Or Col. Sizemore. With him being the new Superintendent, he might not understand like Col. Hartpence did. You could get in trouble."

She was shaking and her face was red. "Just get it and bring it here."

"Well, actually, Mrs. Vincent, you know how you're always getting on us for wearing each other's clothes? You always say, 'Don't wear it if your name isn't on it?' Well, that wine bottle has my name on it. It says 'Gibson's Wine'. So technically, that makes it mine, doesn't it? It does have my name on it."

The girls were all laughing at her. "Go get it, now." She was trembling.

"Well, I'll see if I can find it. If I do, can I have a swig?"

"I don't care. Just bring it here."

Hook chimed in. "How about me? Can I have some?" Several of the girls asked, "What about me? I want to taste it."

I started down the hall with Mrs. Vincent close behind. The girls dropped in line, single file, and marched behind her, imitating her carriage. I went into Hook's room and sat on her bed. I reached in the pillowcase and took out the bottle. I didn't just take it out; I made a big production of it. I slowly turned the cap and said, "Cheers," and took a small sip of the wine. Hook took a sip and passed the bottle to Cheryl. She just looked at it for a few seconds and passed it on to Julie. Mrs. Vincent was standing in the doorway, more upset than I had ever seen her. She snatched the bottle from Julie, pushed the girls out of the way, and walked back to her room. She slammed and locked the door and did not leave her room for the rest of the night. We laughed and talked about her for at least an hour.

But when I went to bed that night, I felt awful. She didn't deserve that. There were a lot of adults at the Home who needed to be humiliated. And I was sure that Mrs. Vincent wasn't one of them.

I never believed that she, Miss Simons, Mrs. Canfield, or Mrs. Atkins, as the only colored supervisors, ever stood up for the colored kids the way they should have. Sometimes, Miss Simons and Mrs. Canfield humiliated us in front of the white kids. The first time anybody called me a spook, it came from Miss Simons, in front of the entire cottage. And she didn't just call me a spook; she called me an ugly, nappy-headed spook. Mrs. Vincent never did anything like that to any of us. She didn't deserve to be humiliated like that. And I never apologized to her. I didn't think I could without crying. And not crying in front of her was far more important than apologizing to her. She didn't punish me for that. And either of us ever spoke about it.

# Chapter 15

༰

The summer before the 11<sup>th</sup> grade was an exciting time for me. About four of us were going away to participate in the Upward Bound Program. Sally Quentin and Charles Potter were going to Wittenberg University in Springfield. Carl Bronson and I were going to Central State University in Wilberforce. We'd be gone for two whole months. The program was set up just like college, except all of our classes would be in the morning. In the afternoons, we'd have special programs or free time.

And we would get an allowance of $100 every two weeks. I couldn't believe it. When I first came to the Home, I was excited when I learned that we got a monthly allowance. At age six, my allowance was 10¢ per month, which the supervisor kept in a jar in her room. As I got older, the allowance increased. At sixteen, my allowance had grown to a whopping total of $1 a month. I couldn't begin to imagine what I would do with $200 a month!

When we got to the campus, we all met in the Student Union. We were assigned roommates and given a tour of the campus. My roommate was Etta Pitts. She was from Dayton.

I was a little nervous, but I thought Etta and I would get along fine.

The next day, we had orientation. We each had to stand in the front of the classroom and say something about ourselves; where we were from, what school we attended, what we wanted to do with our lives, hobbies and interests, and anything else we wanted to say. When I started talking, the giggling began. I heard one of the girls whisper, "What's with the phony accent? Who is she trying to impress?" I was uncomfortable, but I kept talking anyway. Carl got the same thing. I don't know if he heard the comments. If he did, he didn't act as if he did.

There were about 100 kids, all black, from Cleveland, Dayton, Cincinnati, Columbus, and Xenia. They all seemed to know everybody from their own cities. There were at least twenty other kids from Dayton, and Etta knew all of them. There were other kids from Xenia too, but I didn't know any of them. The only person I knew was Carl.

Classes started on the third day. We had three classes a day. At first, I spent most of my free time in my room or I'd hop on Wilbur's bus and ride to town and walk around. Etta and I had really begun to warm up to each other when she had to leave the program. During the third week, three of her friends were killed in a car accident. She said she'd try to come back after the funerals, but I didn't see how she could.

When she left, I stayed to myself. She had been gone about three days, when somebody knocked on my door. I opened it and three of her friends, Ruby and Denise, from Dayton, and Charlene, from Cleveland, were standing there. Ruby said, "Slim, can we come in? We want to talk to you."

I just looked at her and said, "Slim?"

"Yea. That's what Etta called you. Isn't that your nickname?"

"Well, no. Not really."

"Well, whether you knew it or not, Etta called you Slim.

She wasn't trying to be mean, and it does kinda' fit."

I let them in. They all sat on Etta's bed. Ruby continued. "A lot of people think you're stuck up. They think you think you're better that we are. Etta said you're really nice, but you're just shy. She said you're not used to being around black people. Is that true? I mean, where do you live that you've never been around black people?"

We sat and talked for about two hours. I told them all about the Home and my white friends, though I'm sure Etta had already filled them in. They hadn't been around white people much. The public schools system was still segregated, and Ruby said most of them went to all black schools. She said a few of them had white classmates, but they didn't interact with them. Our conversation continued in the cafeteria. Other kids joined us too. Things began to change.

I was one of them. I got invited to parties and dances, though I wouldn't dance. At the Home, I was one of the best dancers, but we didn't dance like these kids. They were moving, and gliding, and doing splits, and stuff I had never seen before. Watching them was better than watching American Bandstand!

Not all of the girls were friendly to me. Some of them still talked about my "phony accent" and thought I was stuck up. Ruby and Charlene became my biggest advocates. They talked to those who really wanted to know why I was so different, and told them about the Home. Some of them viewed me differently and we became friends. Some of them didn't; but it didn't really matter because I had made so many new friends. Etta would have been proud. Ruby, Charlene, and Denise lived up to their promise to her that they would "watch out for me."

On the last night, we had a big dance. We didn't call it a prom, but that's basically what it was. I wore the dress I had worn as Betty's maid of honor in her wedding that summer. The Walker twins from Yellow Springs had convinced their older brother, Thomas, to be my date. I had seen him at Home basketball games when we played Yellow Springs High. He stood out from the other players because one of his arms was shorter than the other and he couldn't straighten it. But it didn't interfere with his game at all.

When Thomas came to the dorm to get me, he had a corsage and a box of chocolates. I got a little teary. My first date. It was just like in the movies! I took the chocolates up to my room and ran back downstairs. Thomas took me by the arm and we walked to the Union. I finally danced. I learned all kinds of new dance steps. I was excited about teaching them to the kids at the Home. And I slow danced with a boy for the first time. I think Thomas was as nervous as I was. He told me he remembered me from the games because I was usually the only black girl on the Home's side of the gym.

When the DJ announced that he was playing the last song, I ran crying to the bathroom. The twins came after me, followed by Ruby and Charlene. Everybody wanted to know if Thomas had done something or said something. I shook my head. "I don't want to go back. I've had more fun during these two months than I've had in my entire life. I don't want to go back to that prison!"

Ruby hugged me. Charlene started to cry. Pretty soon, all of us were crying. Our counselor, Verilyn, wet some paper towels and dabbed at my face. "Come on, honey. You don't want to miss the last dance." She wiped a few other faces too and said, "Ya'll gonna' get me started, and I spent too much time on my make up to be bawling up in here. Now come on." We all laughed.

Thomas was standing near the doorway when we walked out. He held my hand and walked me to the center of the floor and we began to dance. One of the boys tapped him on the shoulder and said, "Excuse me. May I?" A few minutes later, another boy cut in. Nearly every boy in the room danced with me that night. We stayed in the Union long after the dance was over, talking and laughing. I had such a good time.

Thomas walked me back to the dorm. We stood on the porch and talked for a while. He asked if he could kiss me. I don't know why I was so nervous. No, scared was more like it. He could tell that I was uncomfortable, so before I could answer, he kissed me on the cheek and said, "Thanks. I had a really good time." He opened the door and I went inside. He turned and started down the steps. I watched him for a few seconds and opened the door.

"Thanks, Thomas. I had a good time too." He smiled, waved, and continued to his car.

When I got to my room, I changed clothes and started packing. Charlene and Ruby came over. They had a plan. When the bus came for the Cleveland kids the next morning, I could get on with Charlene. Nobody would know. Charlene said her mother would take me in as long as I stayed out of trouble and went to school. It sounded like a great idea, for about ten seconds.

"I can't. Your mother could go to jail."

"But," she replied, "nobody will know where you are. They'll probably be looking in Dayton, where your family is. They'll never think to look in Cleveland."

"Yes they will. They will get the names and addresses of every kid here. They'll find me."

"We could hide you. We know plenty of people in Cleveland. You could rotate, you know, stay with different people every few weeks."

"I can't."

They helped me pack. I had a hard time closing my suitcase. I had spent a lot of my allowance on clothes. I had bought a shirt for Buster, but the rest was spent on me. Emma and I wore the same size and we wore each other's clothes a lot. We were going to look so spiffy in our new outfits.

I really wanted to buy some miniskirts, but I didn't. We weren't allowed to wear them. Our skirts couldn't be above our kneecaps; and depending on the mood of our supervisors or teachers, that might have been too short. Many times, we had to get on our knees. If our skirts were more than an inch from the floor, we were punished. I saved some of the money, but not much. I knew they would take it. They would probably take some of my clothes too; but for some reason, I could accept them taking my clothes easier than I could accept them taking my money.

About seven of us ended up in my room. We stayed up all night, alternating between tears and laughter. We got chips and pop from the vending machines and we talked about everything that had happened over the two months. We talked about our counselors; who was nice, who was mean, and who was dating whom. They talked about their boyfriends back home. We talked about school and clothes and everything teenage girls talk about. I didn't realize it at the time, but we had a slumber party, my very first one.

After breakfast the next day, the buses started lining up in front of the dorms. After Charlene put her suitcases on the Cleveland bus, she came over to me. "Are you sure you don't want to come with me? We can pull this off, you know."

"I want to. I really do. But I just can't."

She hugged me and slipped a folded piece of paper in my hand. "Write me sometime. And if you run away again . . ." She didn't finish her sentence. She didn't have to.

Saying goodbye was hard. This was worse than graduations. A lot of Orphan graduates had younger siblings, so we saw them when they came to visit. And we saw them when they came back for Reunions. The chances of seeing my Upward Bound friends again were virtually nonexistent. And that was hard to accept.

Rev. pulled up in his station wagon. Carl was already in the car and he helped me put my suitcase in the back. I had more slips of paper thrust into my hands and my pockets. Rev. started the car and I got in. It was about a ten-minute ride back to the Home. Rev. asked if we had a good time. Carl said he had. He talked about the classes and the special activities, and the dances. He was still pretty excited. But I didn't say a word.

I thought about Miss Miller and her comments when she took me to St. John's for the first time. "You'll be with your own people. Won't that be fun?"

Until that experience, I didn't really understand what she meant. Sure, we laughed like white people, and we cried like white people. Some of us were smart like white people, and some of us were a little slower, like white people. But there was something uniquely special about being around so many black people. I felt like I had at St. John's, that I belonged. With my white friends, even though I loved them and knew they loved me, there was always a nagging sensation of being slightly on the outside. If a choice had to be made, I was never sure what the determining factor would be: right and wrong, or black and white. I had seen too many instances where black and white was more important than right and wrong. And I'm not sure that my Orphan friends were aware of that, and I certainly didn't bring it to their attention.

With my Upward Bound friends, everything was based on right and wrong. We were all black, so the playing field, in that sense, was level. I finally understood what Miss Miller meant. Being with my own people really was fun.

I had been back for about a month when Bill Garrett came to the Home. I was on duty at the hospital when he walked through the door. I did his lab work and was present when he had his eye exam and his shots. I didn't think he was particularly handsome, though he had pretty black skin. There was just something special about him, something I liked right away. I told Emma about him. She was so happy that finally, I might have a real boyfriend.

A few weeks later, we had the Back-To-School Dance. I hoped he would ask me to dance. When the DJ announced ladies' choice, I went to find him to ask him to dance. I was devastated. June Johnson was sitting on his lap. When she saw me, she kissed his cheek and smiled. I was hurt, but Emma was livid. They both had gone with black boys for a while. Emma had gone with Gary for years, but when they broke up, she dated a couple of other black boys. June dated a few too, some of the same ones Emma did.

Emma and June got into a big argument that night. "You knew Nanny Gib liked him. Why would you do that? You've gone with almost every colored boy in the Home. Do you have to go with him too?"

I was in bed with the sheets pulled over my head. I didn't want Emma to say anything to June. And I didn't want anybody to say anything to me. At that point, it just didn't matter. I was sixteen years old and had never had a boyfriend and I had never been kissed. I didn't count Micky Maxwell. We were only ten years old and our courtship lasted a day and a half. I had resigned myself to the fact that I would never have a boyfriend, and nobody would ever kiss me.

Emma decided that she would break them up. At first, I thought she was doing it so he would be available for me. But once June and Bill broke up, Emma started going with him. They didn't stay together very long. She ended up with Gary again. And when Bill asked me to go with him, I said yes.

We only went to the Saturday night movie together once. And we went on promenade a few times. That's when the boys would come over on Sunday afternoons and we'd walk around the parade field together, holding hands and talking. On our second promenade, he put a ring on my finger, a silver ring with a red stone. We were officially a couple then. We met up at the den a few times, but we never went to the den together. And I think we went to the movie in town once.

Having a boyfriend in the Home pretty much meant smiling at each other and waving when we could in the dining room, at school, or on the playground. Everything else we did, the movies, the den, or promenade, were under the watchful eye of at least four or five adults, so anything more than a quick peck on the cheek was out of the question.

# Chapter 16

ॐ

We were constantly looking for things to do to create some excitement on campus. Our lives were so boring and so predictable. We could look at a calendar, pick a date six months out, and know exactly how the day would go. One night, early in January, Angie, Emma, and I decided to create some excitement. I was still suppose to take elevil and valium four times a day. The last dosage was to be taken at 8:00 in the evening. Since it was dark, girls couldn't walk to the hospital alone. And they didn't want Celeste and me walking together. So they came up with a rotation system. All of the girls in my cottage took turns walking with me to the hospital at night. It was Angie's turn to be my escort. We had decided that since Mrs. Blankenship was on duty, this would be the day to put our plan into action.

Instead of dispensing medications from the clinic, like the rest of the nurses did, Mrs. Blankenship sat in the hall near the east ward. The main door was near the clinic, as was the dispensary, where the medications were kept. After taking my medicine, I started down the hall. As we entered the lobby, instead of going out the door, I ducked into the dispensary, and took a bottle that had about fifteen Ornade capsules in it. Angie and I ran back to the cottage. While the girls were piling into her room to hear of our exploits, I was in the bathroom, emptying the capsules. The girls were calling for me, so I went into Angie's room. All but about three capsules were empty. I started swallowing the empty capsules. Emma, Angie, and several other girls knew the capsules were empty. But Carole didn't. She got scared and ran to get Mrs. Vincent. When she came upstairs, she was so mad.

She snatched the bottle from me and emptied it into her hand. There were three pills left and two of them were still full. I tried to tell her that I had emptied most of the capsules, but she didn't believe me. And she didn't believe that the bottle was only half full when I took it. She took me back to the hospital. Mrs. Blankenship was madder than Mrs. Vincent. Mrs. Blankenship didn't believe me either. She made me drink several pictures of salt water, one after the other. I started vomiting. She called Mrs. Neville.

For the first time, I was beginning to realize how stupid the prank was. Mrs. Neville came to the hospital that night. She never worked at night. As the head nurse, she always worked days, usually 8:00 to 4:00. I tried to tell her what really happened. She didn't believe me. Dr. Olsen came to see me the next day. He didn't believe me. Emma and Angie told Mrs. Vincent and Mrs. Harrigan about the plan, but nobody believed them either. They were just "covering" for me. I was on suicide watch for about three days, then released to my cottage.

About two weeks later, I was called to the principal's office. Mr. Williams told me to go to the hospital. That wasn't unusual. I assumed I needed to do some lab work. When I got to the hospital, Mrs. Neville gave me a pair of pajamas, slippers, a towel and washcloth and told me to change and get in bed. I didn't know why, and no one would tell me.

Mrs. Blankenship was on duty from 3:00 until 11:00 that night. She asked me to pass out the 8:00 medicines. When I was finished, I asked her why I was in the hospital. All she would say was, "Col. Sizemore ordered it. That's all I know." I didn't know whether to believe her or not. Oh, I was sure that Col. Sizemore ordered it, but I wasn't so sure if that was all she knew.

The next day, around 10:00 A.M., Buster came to visit me. That was bizarre. He should have been in school. Visiting hour was between 4:00 and 5:00. He didn't know what was going on either. Then around 1:00, Bill came to see me. That was even more bizarre. He asked for his ring back. "Why?" I asked.

"Just give me the ring, o.k?"

"No. You put this ring on my finger. You take it off."

I thrust my hand at him. He wouldn't look at me. "I don't want to do this. Why won't you just give it to me?"

I didn't say anything. I sat up and moved my hand closer to him. "Take it off! Bill, just take the stupid ring and go."

He took the ring off my hand and kissed my forehead. "I'm sorry. I just don't have a choice."

"Just go. Get out."

He left. About half an hour later, Mrs. Neville came in with my clothes and told me to get dressed. I did as I was told. I went into the hall to see what I was to do next. Mrs. Neville was standing there, along with Miss Bailey, the dentist, the doctor, and another nurse. Mrs. Neville put her hand on my shoulder and looked at me. She didn't say a word; she just looked at me.

"So, what am I suppose to do now?"

Miss Bailey said, "Come with me. I'll tell you about it in the car."

*In the car? Where am I going that she needs to drive me?*

When I got in the car, I noticed two boxes of my clothes in the back seat. She said I was going to Barney Medical Center in Dayton. She wouldn't say why or for how long, even though I asked. She said, "You'll find out why. And as far as how long, I don't know. We'll just have to wait and see."

It was at Barney that I learned that the Home had tried to have me placed at Sciota Village, a juvenile detention center. They refused to take me. There were girls at Sciota who were convicted criminals. The officials there couldn't believe the Home wanted them to take me because I sassed the adults and was belligerent. Then the Home tried to have me committed to Dayton State Hospital, but they refused to take me as well. They agreed that I was defiant, but that was a long way from being mentally ill. After several conferences and a review of my records, one of their psychiatrists recommended placement in a foster home. Dr. Olsen had recommended the same thing, but he was ignored as well. Dr. Olsen knew Dr. Allen, the Chief of Staff at Barney. Upon hearing about me, Dr. Allen suggested that I come to Barney for a complete psychiatric evaluation. *Oh boy, I have really done it this time. Taking those pills was really stupid. I started something now that I can't stop, and it just keeps getting worse. Man, what have I done? What happens now?*

I was in a single room near the nurses' station. I was on suicide watch so the curtains had been removed from my windows.

Barney had never had a physically normal girl of my age as an in-patient. They were not prepared for me. They assumed that the Home had sent everything I needed. The Home assumed that Barney would have everything they didn't send. And nobody thought a physically normal sixteen-year old girl might need sanitary napkins. When I started my period two weeks later, there were no sanitary napkins anywhere in the hospital. My nurse, Mrs. Shelley, gave me an extra large pamper and put a chux pad on my bed. The pamper, of course, wouldn't fit, so I placed it between my legs and didn't move for over an hour. I was so humiliated.

Mrs. Shelley left the hospital and went to the drugstore. When she came back, she apologized and handed me two large boxes of Kotex, a sanitary belt, and a tan stuffed rabbit. She hugged me and apologized again. I showered, made use of my new supplies, and climbed back in bed. I wrapped my arm around my rabbit, pulled the covers over my head, and cried myself to sleep.

◇

Mrs. Neville came to visit me that night. I had never seen her in anything other than her uniform. She was absolutely stunning. She wore a gray, wool coat that had a big fur collar. Her silver gray hair was down and looked so pretty sweeping the collar of her coat. Under her coat, she wore a navy blue, straight dress that accentuated her figure, and navy blue pumps. She had on a single strand of pearls. She was so regal! She told me that she was against the idea of having me sent away. "Whether you believe me or not, I have always liked you. Oh sure, you cut up sometimes, but deep down, I think you're a good kid, a little stubborn, but certainly not crazy."

"What are they going to do with me? How long do I have to be here?"

"I don't know. I'm not privy to that information. And if I were, I'm not sure it would be appropriate for me to discuss that with you."

We visited for about half an hour, then she said she had to go. She put on her coat and walked over to my bed. When she hugged me, I began to cry. "Mrs. Neville, I am not crazy. And I didn't try to kill myself. Those capsules were empty. You have to believe me. Why do you think I took capsules? So I could empty them, that's why. If I had wanted to die, I would have taken the valium or the elevil. And I wouldn't have swallowed them in front of a room full of witnesses. I'm not suicidal and I'm not crazy."

"I know. But what I know and what I believe are not important. You know these decisions are not mine. Now, I have to go. You just," she paused. "Whatever they ask you to do, just do it, honey. You will probably think that some of the tests are stupid, but just take them. Don't say anything, don't ask a lot of questions. Just do what they want. I have to go."

She kissed my forehead and left. She never came to visit me again.

I stayed at Barney for nine weeks. I met with a psychiatrist, Dr. Nancy Paddock, and two psychologists, Pat Maher and Marcia King daily. Pat arranged for me to work with her in play therapy, and to volunteer in the daycare center for children with cerebral palsy. I don't know at what point during my stay that Barney gave the results of my tests to the Home. I do know that they said I was not crazy and that I should be in a foster home, not an institution the size of the OS&SO Home.

One of the reports, written by Miss Hilton, the Home's psychologist prior to my going to Barney stated, "This girl is very much in need of a person with whom she can talk freely . . . and with whom she can eventually learn to express honest anger and honest fear. This she does not yet know how to do. She needs much support and much feeding to help overcome her low self-esteem. It would probably help much if all dealing with her would recognize that her hostility is not a threat to those around her, but rather reveals that she herself feels threatened."

I got mad when I read that. "Low self-esteem." *Is that why I was sent to Barney for nine weeks, because I have low self-esteem? Of course I have low self-esteem. All of us do. Who wouldn't after being treated the way we are? We're told that we are worthless. We're the poor, pitiful little orphans that no one wants. They tell us that we're useless and we'll never make anything of our lives. We're called heathens, imbeciles, morons, niggers, and Lord knows what all. The few possessions we own can be taken from us and given to someone else. Friends are pitted against each other. Siblings are pitted against each other. Sometimes they just disappear, and no one thinks we have a right to know what happened to them. We are emotionally, psychologically, and physically abused. Why would anyone be surprised that we have low self-esteem? I would be shocked to death if any of us don't. And I don't need a degree in psychology to figure that out!*

During the seventh week at Barney, Dr. Paddock told me that I was going back to the Home in two weeks. She didn't agree with that decision, but she couldn't do anything about it. Col. Sizemore wrote to the staff, "The facilities available which would be ideal for Nancy are non-existent at this time. There is some doubt that Nancy could adjust to the responsibilities of a child living at the Home. I am sure that all of us want to do the very best for Nancy and we will use all of the facilities available to us in this adjustment. We realize that time spent at Barney has been well worthwhile and that Nancy is a somewhat improved child over what she was when she left the Home, and is reportedly not as angry or frustrated as she once was."

" . . . a somewhat improved child . . ." That made me mad too. It didn't take a genius to come up with that one. If you keep an alcoholic away from alcohol, he can't drink. Since I was taken away from the source of my anger and frustration, I wasn't angry or frustrated. The people at Barney weren't like the people at the Home. If they asked me a question, they waited for me to answer. I could disagree with them without being called names. I could say "I don't know" if I didn't know something, and nobody hit me in the face with a book. I could talk to them about what happened between my brother and Mitzi and nobody said he was a sex maniac or called her a tramp or a loose trollop.

At Barney, I found people with whom I could "talk freely" and with whom I could "eventually learn to express honest anger and honest fear." I trusted them and they genuinely liked and respected me as a human being. I wasn't used to that and I thrived on that. If the people at the Home were truly sincere about doing what was best for me, they would have followed the recommendations of their own psychiatrist and the recommendations of the highly touted Barney Medical Center and put me in a foster home. They didn't.

At the end of March, I returned to the Home. I went to the hospital first and met with Mrs. Neville and Miss Hilton. Then I went to the cottage where I learned that I would stay downstairs and room with Carole. Then I went to school.

Bill was the first kid I saw. He was leaving the high school building as I was about to enter. He stood on the steps and we looked at each other for a moment. He reached out and hugged me. I hugged him. Neither of us said anything. I know the embrace lasted only a few seconds, but it seemed to last forever. The silence was deafening. He opened the door and I entered the building. He went to the trades building.

I was headed to Mr. Williams's office. Mr. Rooney saw me as I passed his classroom. He stepped into the hall and whispered my name. I turned. He motioned for me to come to him. I did. "How are you?" he asked. He put his hand on my shoulder.

"I'm o.k."

"Are you sure?"

"I guess so. I just don't want to be here."

"I know. But try to make it work, o.k? You have a little over a year left. It's been almost eleven years. Surely, you can make it one more."

"I'll try."

"Good. It's good to see you, dear."

"It's good to see you too, Mr. Rooney."

I went to the office and met with Mr. Williams for about 20 minutes, then I went to class. My classmates were glad to see me and I was glad to see them. I really missed them. The teachers and other adults were so condescending. If they spoke directly to me at all, they did so very softly and slowly, as if I didn't understand English. They acted as if they thought I really was crazy, and no one wanted to be the one to set me off.

The Saturday before my seventeenth birthday, I received a very pleasant surprise. We had just settled down for our afternoon nap. Mrs. Vincent called me and told me I had company. I went into the living room and there sat Pat and Marcia. When I was at Barney, they told me they'd take me out for my birthday. I assumed that promise was good only as long as I was at Barney. I had forgotten they'd even said it. It felt really good to know that there were no conditions on their promise.

We went into town and ate at Frisch's, my favorite restaurant, and went shopping at Singer's, one of the most expensive stores in Xenia. Not many young people shopped there. They couldn't afford to. We got a lot of stares when we walked into the store. I'm sure the sales ladies could tell from the way that I was dressed that I was from the Home and couldn't afford to shop there. And on top of that, I was a black child with two young white women.

Pat bought me a pair of light blue hip-huggers and a dark blue poor-boy shirt. Marcia bought me a green and yellow paisley skirt and a bright yellow poor boy. I was the envy of every girl in my cottage when I walked in carrying two Singer's bags!

Later that month, Marcia took me off campus one evening. In her spare time, Pat was an actress with the Dayton Playhouse. I was surprised that the Home allowed me to go to Pat's play. But soon after, Pat and Marcia were told that it wasn't a good idea for them to visit so much. "We don't want her to get too attached. That wouldn't be good for her. We went through this before with that McDonald family and . . . well, we just think it would be better if you didn't visit so much." They visited a few more times, then their visits stopped.

# Chapter 17

࿐

One Sunday in May 1967, a bunch of us decided that after dinner, we would go to the basement and read and listen to music. Miss Simons had other plans. We were heading down the steps to the basement, when she told us to go outside. Jo said, "But Miss Simons, we wanted to go to the basement and listen to music. We won't play it loud."

She snapped, "You won't play it at all. You're going outside to play."

I said, "Miss Simons, we are seventeen years old. Why do we have to go outside and play like we're ten?"

She responded, "I don't want to hear all that. Go outside. Just go outside."

We were so mad. We stormed outside and sat on the swings and talked about how stupid it was to make us go outside. Somebody said, "If we have to go outside when they want us to, we ought to go out when we want to, like after hours." We sat for a while and plotted about sneaking out.

Jo, Dee, and I went to the square. Jo said, "Were you guys serious about sneaking out?"

Until that moment, I wasn't, but I said, "Sure, why not?"

Dee spoke up. "Count me in. When are we going? What are we going to do?

Jo said, "Let's go tonight."

So, around 10:00 that night, Jo and Dee tiptoed downstairs to my room. We didn't care that it was raining. We were out for some fun. So we crept out my window. First, we went to the grove and picked pears. We ran to the back of the Chapel, sat in the cemetery, ate pears, and told ghost stories. Then we decided to empty the coal bin. That was a complete exercise in futility. We had never really been close to the coal bin before, and had no idea how large it was. It seemed almost as big as our two-story cottage. After dumping coal for about 15 minutes, we decided we'd had enough of that. We hadn't made any real progress anyway.

Jo wanted to go to Roosevelt to see her boyfriend. Dee had a boyfriend in Roosevelt too. I didn't have a boyfriend at all, but three of my best friends, Bobby, Ozzie and Dave, were in Roosevelt. So off we went.

Gerald Barker let us in through his bedroom window. We sneaked upstairs. Jo and Dee went to their boyfriends' rooms, and I went to Bobby's room. About 20 minutes later, we heard that the night watchman was in the cottage. I hid between a six-foot metal storage cabinet and the wall.

The watchman came into Bobby's room with a six-pack of beer. He shared it with the boys. They sat and talked for about half an hour. He sat on Dave's bed the whole time, and never noticed my wet gym shoes beside Bobby's bed. He was too busy drinking his beer and talking about the girls he'd like to feel or kiss or get "under my sheets."

When they were finally able to get him to leave, Dave walked downstairs with him. I sat on Bobby's bed and started putting on my shoes.

He asked, "Do you have to go now?"

I said, "Yea, we'd better get back."

"Can I ask you a question?" He seemed uncomfortable.

"Does it bother you that you don't have a boyfriend?"

"Sometimes."

"Does it bother you that all the colored boys go with white girls? I mean, I know you're not prejudiced or anything, but do you ever get mad about that? You're the only big colored girl. Seems like you could have your pick of the colored boys."

"I guess it bothers me sometimes. I mean, imagine how I felt when they made us go to the Military Ball and Buster was my date. Even Miss Simons was mad about that. Here I am, seventeen years old, and my baby brother took me to the Military Ball. I didn't want to go to the stupid dance in the first place. And I sure didn't want to go with my little brother as my date."

"Can I ask you something else?" He didn't wait for me to answer. "When you went with Bill Garrett, did you guys make out?"

"What? Why do you want to know that?"

"'Cause I heard that he didn't even kiss you. I heard you've *never* been kissed." He waited for me to respond.

I was embarrassed. *Why would Bill tell anybody that he never kissed me?* I hadn't told anybody that, not even Emma. I didn't tell anybody that he did either. I didn't think it was anybody's business. *If Bobby knows, who else knows?*

When I didn't answer, he asked, "Have you ever been kissed?"

I didn't like this conversation. And I was getting frustrated. "No. I've never been kissed, o.k?"

"Since all the colored boys go with white girls, have you ever thought of going with a white boy?"

I really didn't like this. I didn't know what it was leading up to. I knew he wasn't asking about himself. We were close and all that, but I didn't think he would have asked me to go with him. Besides, rumor had it that he and his ex were suppose to be getting back together.

"I don't know. I guess I never really thought about it."

"Do you think you could ever kiss a white boy?"

"I don't know."

He was quiet for a few seconds. Then he said, "Can I kiss you?"

I didn't answer. I didn't know if he had asked because he wanted to kiss me or because he felt sorry for me. I didn't know if I wanted him to kiss me, and I didn't know if I wanted to kiss him. I didn't know what to say.

He rose up slightly on the bed. For the first time, I realized that he didn't have on a pajama top. The light from the hall was just bright enough for me to see how hairy his chest was. My heart was racing and my stomach felt queasy. He put one hand on my cheek and used the other to brace himself in the bed as he leaned forward. He kissed me. It was a soft, gentle kiss. He leaned back and looked at me. I didn't say anything. Neither did he. He sat up and inched closer to me. He put both his arms around me and pulled me close to him. My heart was beating so fast and so hard, I thought I was having a heart attack. His lips were so soft. I could feel his tongue pressing gently against my lips. I didn't know what to do. I opened my mouth just a little and let him put his tongue against mine. *So this is what French kissing is all about!* He began to rub my back. He placed his hand on my side as he pulled back just a little. His hand moved slowly, tentatively under my sweatshirt, up my side, to my breast.

I didn't understand what was happening to me. I had never felt this way before. I felt light headed, as if I were going to faint, and my stomach felt funny. I knew if I stood to leave, my knees would give out and I'd fall to the floor. And I didn't understand why I was so moist between my legs. Then it dawned on me: *This is what the girls mean when they talk about a lubricated kiss!* Suddenly, I was frightened. I pulled away from him.

"I have to go."

"Not now. Please don't go."

"Bobby," I said as I put on my shoe. I didn't finish my sentence. Leaving was the last thing I wanted to do. But I didn't know what would happen if I stayed. I was scared; but I didn't know what scared me more: what he might try, or that I might not stop him.

We heard someone shouting outside. "Chickie! Chickie! If there are any girls in there, get them the hell out of there right now." It was Oscar. He and Jeb had sneaked out and were with Darlene and Cheryl. The night watchman caught them, but he couldn't identify them.

I grabbed my other shoe and ran into the hall. Dee was standing in the doorway. "Where's Jo?" she asked.

I ran down the hall and told Jo we had to get out. We bounded down the steps two and three at a time. When we got to Gerald's room, the screen was still out of the window from where Oscar and Jeb had come back in. There were about eight boys in the room trying to figure out what was going on. Dee went out first. Jo, being ever so dainty, sat on the windowsill and put first one leg up, then the other. I yelled at her. "We don't have time for all that noise. Let's go." I pushed her. I went out the window head first. One of the boys threw my shoe out after me. We took off running. We got back to the cottage and climbed through my window. I wasn't in bed five minutes when Miss Simons got up and made her rounds.

◇

The next morning, Jo, Dee, and I hung our wet clothes on the line in the basement before we went to the dining room. It was at breakfast that we learned that Angie and Julie had sneaked out. They were playing at the greenhouse construction site when they got caught. And true to form, it was Julie's clumsiness that did it. The night watchman was about to leave the greenhouse when Julie sneezed and knocked over a bucket. Also, we learned that Darlene and Cheryl had been making out with Oscar and Jeb in the back of a truck. When the night watchman caught them, the boys threw their shirts over their heads and walked toward him. He yelled at them to get out of the truck. As they neared him, they threw their shirts over his head and told the girls to high tail it out of there. They rolled around in the gravel for a few minutes and the boys grabbed their shirts and ran. He never saw their faces, but he knew one was black and one was white.

That afternoon, a group of boys had to go to the Armory and remove their shirts. Whoever had tussled with the night watchman the night before would have scratches from the gravel. And sure enough, Jeb had marks all over his back and sides. Since there were two of them, and since Jeb and Oscar were always together, they assumed that Oscar was the other boy.

The girls got the usual punishment, confinement to the cottage, fatigue duty in the dining room and the main building. The boys got a little more, though, since they had fought with the night watchman. In addition to confinement, they had to march around the parade field for about two hours, each carrying a rifle horizontally in both hands with their elbows locked.

Nothing was said to or done to Jo, Dee, and me. We figured we'd gotten away with it, though we couldn't imagine how. Saturday was the only day the black girls could press our hair. We sneaked out on a Sunday night, during a rainstorm. I went to bed with straight hair on Sunday night, and woke up Monday morning with an afro! And Miss Simons never said a word.

About ten days later, Mrs. Harrigan came to the cottage. Mrs. Vincent was still on vacation. Mrs. Jamison had replaced Miss Simons as the relief supervisor. Mrs. Harrigan spoke with Mrs. Jamison for ten minutes or so, then she came into the hall and headed toward the living room. She started calling people to the living room. She called for

Darlene and Cheryl; then Angie and Julie. They started toward the door, then she called for Dee, Jo, and me. She said we were going for a little walk.

It wasn't unusual for her to come to a cottage and get girls who had been in trouble and take them to the Gate Store to buy a candy bar, or to Betty's and Bob's Ice Cream Stand. She seemed pleasant enough on our little walk. She asked about school and if we were going home for vacation that summer. She asked if we wanted to go to camp. "Some of you will be seniors next year. Do you plan to go to college?" She kept the conversation going. As we neared the auditorium, she picked up her pace just a little. She was a few steps ahead of us as we approached the gym. Instead of continuing down the hill toward the gates, she turned and headed up the steps leading to the gym. There was no doubt in anyone's mind what was going to happen next.

She stood on one side of the door and Miss Williams stood on the other. "Come on in, girls," Miss Harrigan said with an evil grin.

We entered the gym and lined up under the basketball net. About eight girls from several other cottages were already there. PeeWee was there and so was Mr. Williams. Miss Williams and Mrs. Harrigan stood by the door and chatted briefly, then Mrs. Harrigan came into the gym and said, "Anybody who is not in Taft B, take one step forward." They did. Then she said, "Follow me." They left and went back to their cottages.

Mr. Williams, Miss Williams, and PeeWee whispered among themselves for a few minutes while we stood on the line, not saying a word or moving a muscle. Miss Williams was the first to speak. "So, you can't stay in bed at night, huh? Just can't obey the rules, huh? Have to sneak out after hours, huh? Well, since you have so much excess energy, how about we use some of it up starting right now? That way, when you go to bed tonight, you'll be too tired to even think about sneaking out."

Our first exercise was to run up two flights of steps, cross the balcony, down three flights of steps, cross the basement, then back up to the balcony again. After about the third time, some of the girls started to cry. When we reached the balcony again, I stopped, turned to face the other girls, and said, "Listen. You have to stop crying. Don't you know that's what they want? They want to break us. Don't give them the satisfaction. Just pretend that it's all a big joke. But no matter what, don't let them see you cry. Now come on."

When I turned to start running again, Miss Williams was standing in the doorway. She didn't say anything, but she gave me that look. I expected her to stick out her foot to trip me as I ran past her, but she didn't.

After a few more trips, Mr. Williams told us to line up again. We did. We had to do jumping jacks for ten minutes or so. Then we had to run, as fast as we could, from one end of the gym to the other, slap the wall loud enough for them to hear, then turn and run to the end of the gym and slap that wall. We made about five round trips.

Our next task was to get on the floor and hop like frogs to the other end of the gym until we were told to stop. Most of us had trouble doing that. This wasn't like leapfrog, where we could brace ourselves on someone's back. We were to spring from the floor and hop like frogs. After my first clumsy attempt to hop, my glasses flew off my face. The girls thought that was funny. So did I. Darlene had a hard time with it too. She wasn't the most coordinated person I knew, but I was usually more coordinated than that. Neither of us could get the hang of it. Finally, I said, "Mr. Williams, I don't know what I'm doing wrong, but I can't do this."

He started toward me. "Of course you can." He squatted to demonstrate. "Darlene, you watch this too. Get in this position. And with your hands and feet push off like this. Stretch out your legs a little bit and land like this. Now try it. Both of you."

Darlene said, "O.k. Here goes nothing."

"My glasses keep falling off. Can I put them on the bleachers?" I asked. He nodded. I returned and squatted on the floor and got into the frog position. I was about to spring off when he kicked me, dead center on my rear end. I couldn't believe he kicked me. My first inclination was to get up and punch him as hard as I could.

I stood up and looked him squarely in the eye and said, as if he didn't know, "You kicked me!"

"Yes, I did. Now get down there and do what I told you."

"I will not. I'd have to be a fool or plain crazy to get back down there so you can kick me again. I am not a dog or a foot-stool and your feet don't belong on me. I'll do anything else you want, but I won't get down so you can kick me again."

He hit me so hard he knocked me out. I heard ringing in my ears and everything was pitch black, except for a few flashes of yellow light. When I opened my eyes, he was standing over me, yelling at me to get up. I was flat on my back. I could taste something thick and salty in my mouth. Then I realized that it was blood. I turned my head slightly and saw the other girls standing on the line under the net. Most of them were crying. I could tell that my face was beginning to swell. I tried to get up, but I couldn't. The room was swaying and my legs were like rubber. I fell back down.

I could feel him pulling my hair and tugging on my blouse. When I was back on my feet, he hit me again. As he did, he let go of me and I fell to the floor again. I just lay there, wanting to get up but unable to move. I could see him standing over me and I knew he was yelling at me, but the sounds were muffled and distant. My ears were still ringing, and it sounded as if he were talking in slow motion from another room. When I didn't get up, he grabbed my ankles, dragged me across the floor and flung me in the direction of the other girls. It happened so fast that I couldn't brace myself against the inevitable collision with the gym wall.

He continued to yell at me, telling me to get up. I was finally able to stand, but I felt weak and dizzy. Miss Williams came over and started berating us. "You don't appreciate anything anybody does for you. You poor, pitiful little orphans. Nobody loves you. Nobody wants you. And here you have a nice home, you eat three times a day, you're getting the best education the State of Ohio has to offer, and you don't appreciate it. You just have to have things your way. Want to do what you want, when you want. Well, that's not going to happen. You will do what you're told, when you're told. Ungrateful delinquents. That's what you are. You make me sick. All of you."

By this time, everybody was crying except me. I sure wanted to, but I wouldn't. I couldn't. Our final activity for the night was to hold an industrial-sized dust mop horizontally with both hands, lock our elbows and run laps around the gym. I held mine vertically with one hand and began to jog. Mr. Williams stopped me. "Didn't you understand me?" He snatched the mop from my hand and demonstrated the hold. "You're suppose to hold it like this."

"I can't do that, Mr. Williams."

"And why not?"

"I think you broke my elbow."

I didn't really think it was broken, but it sure hurt like the dickens. He looked at my arm. The look on his face frightened me. For the first time, I looked at my arm. My elbow looked as if someone had peeled back the skin, placed a tennis ball inside, and put the skin back in place. He threw the mop against the bleachers and told me to run. I began to jog around the gym.

He shouted from the sidelines, "Faster. Faster." But I ignored him and didn't break my stride. I had done about five laps when he told us all to stop. The girls piled their mops by the bleachers and we got back on the line. PeeWee paced back and forth in front of us. "You make me sick," he started. Then he stopped in front of me. "And you? You're the most sickening thing I've ever seen. Everybody around here treats you with kid gloves, like they're afraid of you or something. Well, I'm not. I've been waiting to get my hands on you for a long time. And if it were left up to me, this gym would be splattered with your blood and it would take somebody twenty years to find all the pieces of your body. What do you have to say now, big mouth?"

At first, I didn't answer. But he kept on. "I'm talking to you. Answer me!"

I said, "Mr. Edwards, you can kill me if you want. I really don't care. But you will have an awful lot of explaining to do to my father. And I don't think the State of Ohio would take too kindly to you disposing of their property."

His hands moved so fast I don't remember seeing them. I just know that they were around my neck. He backed me into the wall and banged my head against the wall. The thin mat that cushioned the impact of the ball players did little to soften the blows.

Mr. Williams turned to see what was going on. He yelled, "Let her go, PeeWee." When he didn't, Mr. Williams started toward him. "PeeWee, let her go." He walked faster. "Let her go now."

He was standing directly behind PeeWee with the most frightened look I had ever seen on any adult. His hand was on PeeWee's arm, but PeeWee wouldn't let go of me. I couldn't breathe. The room was getting dark and my knees were starting to buckle. Mr. Williams wrapped his arms around PeeWee's waist and spun him around. That broke his grip on my neck and I slid down the wall onto the floor. I don't know how long I lay there. When I opened my eyes, Mr. Williams was bending over me, telling me to get up.

I struggled to my feet and stood on the line with the other girls. After a final lecture from Mr. Williams, they let us go, one at a time, in five-minute intervals. Miss Williams stood in the doorway to make sure we went straight to the cottage and that we didn't stop to wait for each other. I was the last one to leave the gym. Julie had been gone almost ten minutes before I was allowed to leave.

I wasn't sure what they would do next. What had just happened to me was bad, but it wasn't the worst beating that I knew about. I was scared, more scared than I had ever been; but I was determined not to let them know it.

I struggled to control my breathing. I didn't want them to see that 'panic pant' that I could feel welling up. I could feel my heart pounding faster and faster. *Inhale, two... three...four. Exhale, two...three...four. Don't look at them, two...three...four.*

I picked a spot in the middle of the mat on the far wall. As I stared at the mat, I kept telling myself to relax. *Stay calm. Don't you dare cry. No matter what happens next, do not cry!*

Mr. Williams' shoes echoed throughout the gym as he paced the floor. I'd never heard that sound before. We wore street shoes to the basketball games, but the gym was so filled with people and noise that I'd never heard the sound of footsteps in the gym. At least, I never paid any attention to the sound. It sounded a little eerie.

Suddenly, it was quiet. He had stopped pacing. Now I was terrified. As long as he was moving, I thought I could relax a little. But now that he had stopped, I didn't know what to expect.

I could feel PeeWee standing near me, staring at me. I truly believed, and still do, that if he could have gotten away with it, he would have killed me that night.

Mr. Williams finally spoke. "Go on. Get out of here."

I felt a small sense of relief. I couldn't totally relax because there was still time for his sister or PeeWee to do something. I started toward the bleachers.

PeeWee yelled, "The door is the other way, stupid. Where do you think you're going?"

I turned and completely ignored him. "Mr. Williams, I know where I'm going, but I need to see to get there. Do I have your permission to get my glasses off the bleachers so I can see to get back to the cottage?"

He didn't look at me. "Get your glasses and get out of here."

I got my glasses off the bleachers and put them on. The left side of my face was so swollen that I could feel the bottom of the frames pressing against my cheek. Miss Williams was still standing in the doorway with the door open. As I started down the steps, she closed the door. "Well, you're a pretty tough cookie, huh? Nobody can get to you, huh? Nobody can make you cry, huh? Well, little girl, you're not as tough as you think you are."

I didn't respond. I just stared straight ahead.

She continued. "Oh, you don't have anything to say? You, with all the mouth don't have anything to say?"

I answered. "At the risk of being beaten again, I do have something to say, Miss Williams." I turned and looked at her. "I may not be as tough as I think I am, but I'm a whole lot tougher than you think I am."

Her fist flew into the air, ready to come down hard against my already swollen cheek. I heard Mr. Williams shouting from behind me. "Don't do it, Lizzie." Her hand hung in the air as she looked up the steps at her big brother. "Lizzie, don't. Let her go. Just let her go!"

She looked at him for a few more seconds. Her hand slowly dropped to her side and she opened the door. "Get out of here. The very sight of you just makes me sick."

I looked at her again and said, "Good night, Miss Williams," and I walked out. She stood in the doorway and watched as I headed up the hill. I made it just past the auditorium when the tears started to flow. But I didn't make a sound. I couldn't make a sound or she'd hear me, and that just would not do.

◇

When I got to the cottage, all the girls were in my room. Some were piled on Carole's bed, some were on mine, some were on the floor, and all of them were crying. Emma was the first one to get to me. She hugged me and all the tears that I hadn't cried for years came pouring out on her shoulder. She walked me over to the bed, and we just sat, hugging each other, and crying. Somebody was touching my leg. Somebody else was patting my arm. Somebody was stroking my head. It was as if all the girls in that room needed to touch me, to reassure themselves that I was still alive.

The girls who were in the gym kept apologizing. Darlene said, "I'm sorry, Nancy. I wanted to do something. I wanted to help you, but . . ." The words were suspended, just hovering there in the room, unfinished.

I wanted to ask her, to ask all of them, *Why didn't you? I wouldn't have done that. I couldn't have stood there and watched anybody do to you what they did to me. There were seven of us and only three of them. And we're suppose to be friends, sisters. Why didn't you do something?*

But I knew why. They were terrified. Their whiteness did not exempt them from abuse. They had seen and been subjected to as much violence as I had. Besides, what could they have done that wouldn't have made matters worse for all of us? They felt bad enough. So I didn't say anything. I just cried harder.

Mrs. Jamison didn't know what to do. She had fourteen hysterical teenage girls on her hands. She told Emma and Carole to get dressed and walk me to the hospital. My gym partners said they were going too. She told them to go to bed.

Angie said, "No, we'll take her. We started this night together. We're going to finish it together."

They helped me to my feet and we left the cottage. It took Mrs. Jamison some time to get the other girls to calm down and go back to bed. Then she went to Monroe A, where Mrs. Kelley had a telephone. She called Mr. Williams and told him what was going on. He called the hospital and told Mrs. Blankenship that we were on our way and that we should all sit in the lobby until he got there.

When we arrived, Mrs. Blankenship didn't get up from the desk. She told us to sit down and be quiet and she split us up. We were still crying, though I made no sound. I sat on the couch near the office and could see out the front window. I saw Mr. Williams as he came up the sidewalk. I wiped my face and the tears stopped flowing. He lectured us about obeying the rules and said, "Now, the excitement is over. Everybody go back to the cottage, except Nancy."

The girls turned and looked at me. I just sat there, staring straight ahead, not moving, not doing anything to let him know how much I hurt and how scared I really was. They left reluctantly. He got the key to Mrs. Neville's office from Mrs. Blankenship and motioned for me to follow him. He sat behind the desk and told me to sit down. I sat in the chair nearest the door.

"Are you all right?" he asked.

I laughed. "Am I all right? Yea, I feel fine. I mean, when I went to the cottage after dinner, I said to myself, 'Man, if somebody would just beat me up tonight, if somebody would just knock me around like I'm a worthless piece of garbage, my life would be complete.' And lo and behold, that's exactly what happened. Yep, life is great. I don't think it gets any better than this."

He slammed his fist on the desk. "See, that's why people react the way they do. You have entirely too much mouth."

"Well, Mr. Williams, when I was in Peter Pan, it was drilled into my head that if you ask a stupid question, you should expect a stupid answer. How do you think I feel? Do you really think I'm all right?"

He didn't answer right away. In a much softer tone he said, "You and I have always gotten along. I've always been fair with you. At least, I've always tried to be. There have been many times when I should have punished you and didn't. I don't know why you act this way. You make people not like you, then you blame them. Why do you push people to the limit? Why did you push me? Why did you make me hit you?"

I just shook my head. And I thought, *Man, this sounds familiar.* I gave him the answer I wanted to give to Miss Allen, Miss Miller, Belinda Logan, Peter Boles, and a host of others after they beat me or threw things at me. It was a common question, one that had been asked of me and far too many Orphans far too often. I finally answered. "Mr. Williams, you are a grown man. I am a seventeen-year old girl. I'm not in charge of anything at the OS&SO Home. How can I *make* you do anything?"

"I see this conversation isn't going anywhere. We all know that you have problems. Everybody thinks that you need a rougher hand to make you toe the line. But I always thought a softer approach would work better, might bring you around. I've tried. But tonight, you just threw all of that back in my face. Maybe they were right all along. Maybe I was mistaken."

I couldn't believe my ears. *I'm the one with the tennis ball-sized elbow. I'm the one with the busted mouth and the swollen face. I was kicked, knocked out, and choked. Maybe I'm stupid, or maybe I really do have a problem, because I just can't see how you're the injured party here.*

He told me that I was staying in the hospital for a few days, until things calmed down. "Go see Mrs. Blankenship and get some pajamas." As I stood to leave he said, "Good night, Nancy."

I looked at him and replied, "It is night. I wouldn't go so

far as to say it's been a good one though." Then I walked out. Mrs. Blankenship told me to get some pajamas and get changed. I was fine until I got to the bathroom. I slid down the wall to the floor and began to cry. Mrs. Blankenship finally came down the hall and when she saw that I wasn't in bed, she came into the bathroom.

"Come on, get up and change your clothes." She took me by the arm. When I looked up at her, she said, "Oh my God." She scared me. I hadn't seen my face yet. And after her reaction, I was afraid to look, but I did.

I turned slowly and looked in the mirror. The left side of my face was swollen and red. The right side of my face was swollen near my mouth and down to my chin. Dried blood was smeared at the corner of my mouth and stained the front of my shirt. Welts, in a perfect pattern of PeeWee's hands, adorned my neck. I looked awful. And I knew that when the redness turned to bruises, I'd look worse.

She wet the wash cloth and wiped the blood from my mouth. Her eyes brimmed with tears. "You didn't deserve this," she said. "Oh sure, you can be stubborn as a mule, a real handful sometimes, but you didn't deserve this." She left. I put on the pajamas and got into bed. She came back with an ice pack, but it just made my headache worse so I put it on the table.

She stayed in the room for a few minutes without either of us saying a word, then she left again. I was so empty. I couldn't cry anymore. I just lay on my side, and sobbed, but there were no tears. They just wouldn't come.

I thought of Rita McGregor and how, after her gym party, her mother came and took her home. They just packed Rita's bags and they left. I wanted somebody to come get me. I wanted my mother. I needed her to hold me and tell me that she loved me, and that everything would be fine.

I stared at the doorway, as if at any minute, she'd come for me. And then I realized that if she did, I probably wouldn't recognize her. I couldn't see her face anymore. I couldn't remember what my mother looked like and I couldn't remember what she sounded like. I could only remember that she was short, and round, and soft.

And I longed for a blue popsicle. I hadn't wanted one or thought about one in years. I wasn't even sure they still made them. I reached up and took the ice pack off the bedside table. I opened it and took out a small piece of ice. I put the ice in my mouth, wrapped my arms around myself, and rocked myself to sleep.

◇

By breakfast, word about what happened was all over campus. Miss Olivia was on maid service at the hospital. I had never really liked her very much. She never really liked me either. Anyway, she came into the room in the morning and walked straight to my bed.

She said, "Turn over. I want to see what all the fuss is about."

I didn't say anything and I didn't move.

She said it again. I still didn't answer or move. She came around to the other side of my bed. She pulled the covers back and gasped. "Oh, my Lord Jesus. Who did this?"

I wouldn't talk to her.

"They said Mr. Williams beat you up, but I didn't believe it. I've known that man for years. He wouldn't do this. He *couldn't* do this!"

I was mad. I said, "He *could* do this. He *would* do this. And he *did* do this! Now, leave me alone." I pulled the covers back over my head.

As she left the room, I heard her mumbling to herself. The only thing I heard clearly was, "We'll see about this."

I was right. When I got up to wash for breakfast, my face looked worse than it had the night before. I stayed in the hospital for a couple of days, until some of the swelling went down. Neither my friends nor my brother were allowed to visit me. Nobody talked to me about what happened, not even Mrs. Neville. They all acted as if things were normal, as if nothing happened at all.

I left the hospital right after breakfast on Saturday morning. It was good to be back in the cottage with my friends. Mrs. Vincent was back from vacation. She was furious when Miss Simons told her what happened. I was surprised to learn that Miss Simons was mad too.

On the way to the cottage after lunch, I saw my brother's car. Ben, who by now had changed his name to Reco, yelled for me to get in the car.

"I can't. I'll get in trouble with my supervisor."

He yelled back, "Would you rather be in trouble with her or with me? Now get in the damned car!"

I did what he said. I didn't ask him how or when he found out what happened. He was too mad for that. "Look at me," he demanded. "Who the hell beat you up like that?"

"Mr. Williams."

He started the car. "You tell me everything that happened. From the time you left the cottage to the time you got back. I want to know who said what and who did what. And don't you leave out anything, do you hear me? Start talking." He parked the car behind the trades building, near the auto shop. I told him everything. The more I talked, the madder he got.

"Now, you're telling the truth? You're sure it was Mr. Williams?"

*Why does everybody keep asking me that?* "No, Reco, it wasn't him. I'm just making it up." He looked at me. "Of course it was Mr. Williams. I know who hit me. I'm not stupid. And I'm not a liar. Why would I say it was him if it wasn't?"

"I know you're not stupid, baby, and I know you're not a liar. I just can't believe it was him. I really like him, and I can't say that about many people up here."

"Well, I liked him too, right up 'til the minute he kicked

me. And the strange thing is, I think I still like him." I could feel the tears beginning to well up. "Reco, do you think I'm crazy? I'd just about have to be to like somebody who did this to me, huh?"

"Naw, baby, you ain't crazy. But I'll tell you this," he put the car in gear. "He damn sure must be if he thinks I'm gonna' sit still for this."

"Where are we going?"

"We're going to Williams' house. Don't you open your mouth or say a word until I tell you to, do you understand me?"

"Yes."

I'm sure Mr. Williams was expecting us. When we arrived at his house, his kids were nowhere to be found. Reco knocked on the door. Mrs. Williams told us to come in. He was sitting in an easy chair, and she was sitting on the arm of the chair. They looked as if they were posing for a portrait. After they exchanged the customary "hello's and how do you do's" Reco said, "We need to talk. I've known you for a long time. I've been a guest in your home. I've eaten at your table and slept here many times." That came as a surprise to me. I had no idea Reco had been their house guest.

He continued, "Now, I've already talked to my sister and she told me what happened. Now, I'm going to ask you the same thing. What happened?"

Mr. Williams proceeded to tell his version of the story. Basically the story was the same up to a point, though he did say I refused to do the frog leap, not that I had problems doing it. Then his story got really bizarre. He proceeded to talk about how I was being difficult, and how they lectured us and then we went back to the cottage. At no time did he indicate that anyone kicked me, hit me, or choked me.

Reco started getting mad again. "Who the hell beat her up like this?"

"Now Ben, I don't think I'd say that anyone beat her up.

I may have slapped her once. Isn't that right, Nancy?"
I didn't answer him. Reco hadn't said I could talk. He asked me again. Reco looked at me and said, "Well?"
Then I started talking. "Mr. Williams, you left out the part where you kicked me. And no, you didn't slap me once. You punched me in my face twice. And you pulled my hair, and you dragged me across the floor and threw me into a brick wall. Did you forget that? And did you forget that PeeWee choked me and that you kept your sister from punching me in the jaw."
"Now Nancy, there's no need to exaggerate."
I pulled the collar on my blouse down. "Does this look like an exaggeration to you? These are real bruises from real hands, PeeWee's hands. There were eight other people in that gym besides you and me. I know for a fact that at least six of them will tell the truth to whoever asks."
Reco told me to be quiet. "I've heard all I need to hear. Mr. Williams, I've always respected you. I've always thought you were fair. There aren't many people I can say that about. But regardless of what I think of you, this is my sister, my baby sister. You, or nobody else can get away with beating her like this."
Mr. Williams interrupted him. "Now Ben, . . ."
But before he could say anything else, Reco said, "That's o.k. Mr. Williams. I don't have anything else to say. We're leaving now. And the next time you hear about this, it'll be from my lawyer. I suggest that you get one too. I'll see you in court." He took me by the hand, pulled me up from the couch and we walked out.
I never did ask Reco how he found out.

The Superintendent called an emergency meeting of the Board. I was summoned to the Main Building. They asked me what happened and I told them. Then Mrs. Lowe, the only black and the only woman on the Board, said, "I understand, from our other interviews, that you have been a trouble maker for some time. Don't you think Mr. Williams was justified in chastising you?"

I just sat for a moment, then very calmly, with absolutely no emotion said, "Perhaps if I had been chastised, I might think so. But I wasn't chastised. I was kicked like a dog and beaten and choked. My life was threatened. No, I don't think that was justified. And if you think that is proper chastisement for a child who can't hop like a frog, trouble maker or not, then maybe there's something wrong with you."

I was asked a few more questions. What did I want to come out of this? Did I want to leave the Home? Did I want to stay in the Home? If I stayed in the Home, did I want my brother and sister to pursue the court case?

"You're asking me what I want. Hmm. Let me see."

I paused for a minute, then I continued. "I will never forget my first day in the Home. I was only six years old, and I was scared. My mother had died six months earlier, and I went to live with Miss Jenkins, a woman I didn't know, and I was afraid of her. A few months later, I came here, and everything about this place and everybody in it scared me. My sisters and I were in the Snow White room in the hospital and I was scared of that witch on the wall. No matter which bed I tried, that witch kept scowling at me. I was scared to death that the witch was going to get me. I wanted to move to another room."

They looked at each other in utter bewilderment as I kept talking. "When the nurse came to check on us, my sister, Betty, told her we had to move. She said, 'My little sister can't sleep in here. She's scared of the witch.' The nurse made it very clear that we had to stay where we were. In a cold, abrupt tone she said, 'Children don't make the decisions here at OSSO. It doesn't matter what she wants.'

"So, to answer your questions Mrs. Lowe, quite frankly, it doesn't matter what I want. It never has and it never will.

I'm sure you will do exactly what you want. Considering the wants and needs of a poor, pitiful little orphan. . . well, that just isn't the way things are done at the OSSO. Now, may I be excused?"

They just looked at each other, then at me and Mrs. Lowe said, "You're excused."

# Chapter 18

Bobby had been ignoring me at school. I wasn't sure why. One day, I cornered him. "Listen, if you're afraid I told somebody about what happened between us, don't be. I didn't tell anybody. I wouldn't do that."

He just looked at me. "I know that."

"Then what's wrong? Why are you avoiding me?"

"I'm just having some trouble with the guys, that's all."

"Why?"

"Because they think I told on you guys."

"Who thinks that?"

"Everybody. They say that if I had kept my big mouth shut, nobody would ever have known that you were out, and you wouldn't have been beat up."

"Who's everybody?"

"Dave, Ozzie, everybody. Nancy, I didn't tell on you. I wouldn't tell on anybody, especially not you."

"I know that." I felt so sorry for him. "Don't you worry. I'll talk to Dave."

I waited in the hall for Dave as we switched classes. He could tell I was mad about something. "What wrong, Nancy?"

"Why are you guys messing with Bobby?"

"That rat fink. He went crying to you?"

"Are you messing with him or not?"

"Yea, after what he did, he deserves to be messed with and messed up."

"Dave, he didn't do it. Bobby Wade would never tell on me. Not in a million years."

"Well, somebody squealed."

"But it wasn't him. You're messing with the wrong person. Leave him alone."

"Well, there's a rat fink in Roosevelt and everybody thinks it's him."

"Well, everybody is wrong. Stop messing with him."

"Well, all right. But I'm going to find out for sure who the fink is. If it's not him, I'll apologize. But if it is, he ain't seen nothing yet."

"It's not him. Trust me."

Over the course of the next few weeks, several rumors were circulated, naming people who supposedly told. We never did find out for sure who it was, but I always knew that it wasn't Bobby Wade.

◇

I was to leave the Home in early June. Betty had graduated from nursing school and had an apartment in Xenia. I would live with her. I didn't even get to stay for graduation. There were kids in the graduating class I had known since Peter Pan. And, of course, there were my classmates. Most of us had been together from the beginning. We'd been through eleven years of ups and downs, good times and bad times; and now that we were down to the wire, one more year to go, I was leaving.

Shortly after Betty and Dean left, I had resigned myself to the fact that I would never leave the Home early. I'd have to graduate. I had finally accepted that reality, and now it was being changed.

And poor Buster. He was the last one of us left. We always knew he would be the last one, but if I graduated, at least he would have time to prepare himself for his last two years alone. This way, he didn't have any advanced notice. He found out the same day I did. I was excited, yet apprehensive.

When I told my friends, they all cried. The hard part was telling them that I couldn't come on campus for three months, and then, only if Betty came with me. And if I wanted to see them, they'd have to visit with me in the main building. I couldn't walk the campus or sit in the open spaces like other visitors. Even though I'd no longer be "state property," the state would be running my life still.

When the day to leave finally came, I was terrified. But I put on a good show. I didn't want to upset the other girls and I didn't want them to know how utterly terrified I really was. And I most definitely couldn't let any of the adults see the slightest indication of my fears. I was afraid of what was out there. *What if I find that the adults out there are no different from the adults in here? What if everybody acts this way? What if my teachers at Xenia High School tell me how worthless I am and that I will never amount to anything? What if I say the wrong thing in class and a teacher hits me or calls me a dunce or an idiot? What if they're right? What if I really am the one with the problem?*

After all those years of trying to break me, they finally succeeded by giving me the one thing I had asked for, that I had longed for, that I had prayed for. I was leaving the Home, and I'd finally have a chance to be me. Not the cookie-cutter automaton they tried to make me. Not the submissive, compliant child they wanted, who didn't react to the insanity that filled every facet of my life. Not the unquestioning teenager who witnessed and experienced all manner of abuse, yet was expected to remain deaf, blind, and mute. I was finally getting a chance to live a normal life. The problem was, I didn't know what normal meant.

After lunch, the parade to my room began. We all cried and hugged each other. I loved my friends. Saying goodbye to them would be hard. But saying goodbye to Emma would be the hardest of all. Eleven years. That's how long we had known each other. That's how long we had been friends. She was my sister. We made a blood oath when we were seven years old. We took a straight pin and pricked our left index fingers. We squeezed the tips of our fingers until we saw a bead of blood. We pressed our fingers together, mixing our blood, and vowed to be sisters forever. We rubbed our blood on the straight pin, and buried it by the tree near the sandbox. And from that day on, we were officially related.

We had shared so many secrets and sorrows, so many laughs, so many tears, both sad tears and happy tears. Who else could I wake up in the middle of the night to listen to a poem I had just written? Who else would stay up with me all night to guard the window because one of the employees told my brother that I was "stacked up" and he was going to sneak into my room to "get some."

Who else could she talk with about her trials and travails with Gary? Who else could she share her deepest pain with when her foster mother disowned her because she went steady with a colored boy? I didn't want to tell Emma goodbye. I couldn't. And technically, I didn't. When she came into my room, she plopped on my bed. We hugged each other so hard we fell back on the bed and lay there and cried.

When Betty came to get me, we loaded my things in her car. On my final trip to the cottage to get the last of my belongings, everybody was standing in the hall. As I left the cottage for the last time, I didn't say goodbye. All I could say was, "O.k you guys," and I left. I got in the car. I couldn't turn around to wave. I was afraid that if I did, I'd jump out and beg Mrs. Vincent not to make me go. As Betty started the car, I buried my face in my hands and began to cry. I was about to take the most important step of my life;

the first step in a very long journey; the journey to me.

The trial was an absolute farce. I had no expectations of fairness. I had learned a long time ago, that fairness is determined by the person in control. I wasn't in control; therefore, my definition of fairness meant nothing. I sat in that courtroom for five days and listened as witness after witness took the stand and told the most bodacious lies about me.

Teachers, whose classes I never took, testified about what an obnoxious, disruptive student I was. Mrs. Collins, one of the few teachers I liked, testified about a fight we never had. It was my sister, Dean, who slapped her. Supervisors testified that I was unwilling to do the simplest chores around the cottage and that I made the other girls make my bed and wash my dirty clothes. Mrs. Jamison testified that there were no bruises, swelling, or any other marks on my face and neck. She said that when I came into the cottage, I was laughing and joking with the other girls, and that I got upset only after she told us to go to bed. Nobody, except the six girls with me that night, recalled seeing any bruises or blood, not even Mrs. Blankenship.

And the testimony of the girls was discounted because I was manipulating them. Col. Sizemore said they were afraid of me and would do anything I told them to do. I had been out of the Home for about six weeks when the trial began. I hadn't spoken to any of them since I left. I didn't understand how I was manipulating them. Mind control, I guess.

He also testified that I was failing every subject except drama, at which I was very good and used to control and manipulate people. I wanted to speak up. *Failing every subject? You big liar! I've never gotten a D or an F in anything! If my grades were so bad, why hadn't I repeated a grade? And why wasn't my name ever on the D & F List that was published and posted on the bulletin board in each cottage so everybody would know who was failing what?* I just sat there and listened as he continued to fabricate the most unbelievable tales. He said I was an "insolent, incorrigible ingrate, who didn't appreciate the hard work of good people who tried to provide a good home" for me.

And, according to the definition accepted by the Home, the Board of Trustees, and the State of Ohio, Mr. Williams hadn't kicked me at all. Their definition of a kick was "to hit a person or an object with the toe of the shoe so as to cause harm or injury." Mr. Williams didn't intend to cause any harm, and he used the instep of his shoe, not the toe; therefore, he hadn't really kicked me. Col. Sizemore said that I "had deliberately twisted a friendly boot to the seat as a slap in the face, when in fact, it was the OS&SO Home that had been slapped in the face by an ungrateful, ill-tempered, belligerent girl."

Dr. Olsen was on Mr. Williams's witness list. If he testified, I would have to leave the courtroom. I wouldn't agree to that. There was never anyone else present during any of our sessions. I wanted to hear what he would say, in case I needed to refute it. As much as I liked him, I didn't trust him. He was, after all, on the Home's payroll.

Dr. Paddock, the psychiatrist from Barney, was on my witness list. She had seen me one week after the incident and I still had bruises. That was to be the extent of her testimony.

Mr. Williams's lawyer said, "If Dr. Paddock testifies, Dr. Olsen testifies." The judge agreed.

I couldn't imagine what might come pouring from Dr. Olsen's mouth. As strong a witness as I thought Dr. Paddock would be, I didn't think her testimony alone would be enough to level the mountain of lies that had already been told. It was too big a risk. I refused to let Dr. Olsen to testify; therefore, Dr. Paddock didn't testify either.

Mr. Rooney was called as a witness too. I felt sorry for him. He was uncomfortable and everybody knew it. Of all the witnesses they called, he was the only one who told what he knew, what he saw, and what he heard first hand. He also said I was a good student, one of his best. He said I was smart and talented and that he hadn't seen the "incorrigible kid" everybody else saw. His testimony didn't really help me, but it didn't hurt me either.

But I guess what hurt me most was that neither Daddy nor Miss Jenkins came to the trial. Neither of them came to see me after the beating either. They relied on status reports from Betty and Reco. And I guess they got status reports about the trial from Betty and Reco too, if they were interested at all, because neither of them ever spoke with me about it.

We didn't win. I didn't expect to. I didn't agree to pursue the case for myself. I did it for Buster and for my friends, the kids who were still there and still being abused. What I wanted from the case, all I ever wanted, was for the brutality to stop. Kids had their noses broken at the hands of teachers or needed stitches to close wounds from being hit with boards and paddles. Kids were stripped naked, scrubbed with brushes and laundry soap, and rinsed off with garden hoses, while everybody in their cottages was forced to watch. We suffered all manner of indignity, humiliation, and outright abuse. I was tired of it. If someone had sued before, maybe I wouldn't have been subjected to such outrageous violence under the guise of discipline.

I was no angel. I talked back and spoke up when I knew it was better to remain silent. I was deliberately impish at times and pulled pranks that I knew were inappropriate. I was stubborn and unbending when it came to what I believed to be right or true. I made absolutely no effort to become the docile, submissive, blindly obedient child they wanted me to be. But I do not, and never will believe that I did anything that would justify the beating I endured that night in the gym.

Some people tried to make it a racial issue. And for a brief time, I entertained the possibility too. But as I thought about it more and more, I discounted that. Some of the adults were closet racists and would deny that there was anything racist about them or their behavior. Others were openly hostile toward black kids and didn't care who knew it. I had been in the Home one month short of eleven years. Surely, I would have seen or heard something that would have indicated that Mr. Williams was a racist. There were plenty of adults who were. I just didn't believe that he was.

I had always admired him. And that's what made the situation so difficult to accept and to understand. If Miss Williams or PeeWee had beaten me, it wouldn't have been so emotionally devastating. It wasn't that I hated either of them. But if they had suddenly dropped off the face of the earth, it wouldn't have fazed me one bit. And it was quite obvious to everybody that they felt the same about me. But coming from Mr. Williams, the assault was a shock, not only to me, but to just about everybody else as well. It was so out of character for him.

I tried to fathom what I had done that was so terrible that somebody, anybody, would think that it was appropriate to use me as a punching bag. I stewed over what I had done that caused him to snap. But I couldn't think of anything. It saddened me to finally realize that I wasn't beaten because of something I had done. I was beaten because of something I wouldn't do. I was beaten because I wouldn't bend, and I was beaten because I wouldn't break.

# Chapter 19

ॐ

This journey has taken a long time. It has not been an easy trip. I guess I didn't really understand how my experiences as an Orphan would have such a profound impact on the rest of my life. I spent a lot of time wondering why. *Why did this happen? Why did God allow this to happen to me?* Sometimes I cursed God and questioned His existence.

Unknowingly, I wore my wounds as a badge of survival. And because they were wounds, open, festering sores, I was in constant pain. I had to learn, as an adult, that my thoughts and opinions mattered. I had to re-learn, as an adult, that I am valued, not for what I do, but for who I am. I learned that from Sis. Walker when I was six years old. But somewhere along the way, I began to question the validity of that.

Then one day I realized that the problems were not with me or my friends, but with those who were responsible for us. We were children. No child deserves to be treated the way we were. On a conscious level, we all know that. But on a deeper, subconscious level, there was a part of me that wondered if there might be something inherently unworthy about me. I wondered if there was something in me, that others saw, that was innately evil. The name calling, the beatings, and the abuse had taken a toll. And if the intent was to make me question my value and my worth as a human being, then I'd say they almost succeeded.

But I made a conscious decision to be me. After all those years of running and hiding, I finally faced what I feared most, finding and being me. And in the process, I decided to change my name as well. I had wanted to change my name for a long time. I wanted an African name. When I was a baby, Reco named me after a nappy-headed white girl in the funny papers. Nancy was what I had been called, but Nancy was never who I was. And the Nancy I knew did not exist anymore. I was somebody else now, and wanted a name that was more reflective of the person I had become and how I chose to live. I refused to be called by a name that wasn't mine. So in 1987, while visiting The Gambia, West Africa, I participated in a name-changing ceremony. I chose my own name, a name that meant something to me: NeAnni Yakini Ife: wealth, truth, love.

And I continue to make changes in my life as well. I discovered that being me was a good thing. I think Ntozake Shange said it best when she wrote, "I found God in myself, and I loved her. I loved her fiercely." I could no longer live buried behind a facade or hiding in a shell. I had lived as a turtle long enough.

The realization and the subsequent transformation were not instantaneous. It wasn't like Jack and his magic beans and overnight, I was a new me. It took a long time and a lot of validation that I didn't know I needed. Through the nurturing of my mother/sister/friend, I came to believe and to understand that I am, as the Bible says, "fearfully and wonderfully made." I had to strip away layers of lies and decades of doubt that had become so much a part of my life that I couldn't decipher what was real. I had relied on my talents as a writer to create a persona, and my abilities as an actress to become that character.

How I wish I had come to that decision much earlier. It would have made such a difference in the choices I made and in the way I raised my children. I was strict with them, probably more strict than I needed to have been. I did the best I could with what I had and with what I knew.

Mothering them was the most rewarding thing I have ever done. I tried to be the mother to them that I always wanted. For the most part, I think I was successful at that. They are now in their early 30's and both are so talented and funny, smart, happy, and healthy, and they know that they are loved and appreciated for who they are.

In 1997, I quit my job, left my house, my son, my siblings, and my friends, and moved to Virginia. At the time, my daughter was the only person here that I knew. I had no job and no prospects lined up. It was a bold move. Some people said I was having a mid-life crisis. Some said I was crazy, but that didn't bother me. I'd heard that before. But I needed a change. I didn't know if it would be for the better; I just knew that I needed to do it.

During my second week in Virginia, I had an experience that would forever change my life. It was on July 14, 1997, a beautiful, sunny, Saturday morning. My daughter sang with her church choir. I was accompanying her to rehearsal, after which we were to ride around so I could become familiar with my new surroundings.

While we were on Route 1, about three miles from the church, a deer bolted from the woods and stopped in the middle of the road. Miraculously, no one hit it. The deer was frozen in fear and just stood there for about thirty seconds. Then she turned slightly, ran, and attempted to jump over the railing on the right side of the road. She missed and crashed through the windshield of my daughter's car, and landed on my lap.

I was unable to move. Other drivers and passengers got out of their cars and stood there yelling, "Oh my God! She's got a deer on her lap." My daughter got out of the car and pleaded, "Somebody help my mommy. Please, somebody help my mommy."

I was covered with blood, some from the deer and some of my own. I had shards of glass in my hair, face, and eyes. And I was hysterical. A man opened the passenger door. He reached into the car, grabbed the deer by the neck, pulled it out, and threw it on the side of the road.

His name was Jack Mitchell. He knelt beside the car and held my hand. He picked shards of glass from my face. He told my daughter to get a towel or something to stop the blood from flowing from my head. He comforted both us and reassured both of us that I would be fine. He didn't let go of my hand or leave my side until the paramedics arrived.

It's hard to believe that both my daughter and I walked away from that accident with minor injuries. My daughter had a small cut on her right hand, and I had a small cut on my forehead. The nurses, the doctors, the X-ray technicians, none of them could believe that nothing was broken. Even the police officer stopped by to see me to tell me how lucky I was to have survived.

The week before and for several weeks after, the newspaper carried stories about people who had been killed in accidents with deer. I began to realize how blessed we were. I thought about Jack Mitchell, and how calm he was while everyone else panicked and didn't know what to do. This man whom I didn't know and haven't seen since, knelt beside the car and held my hand and comforted me during one of the most frightening experiences of my life.

The week after the accident, I went to church with my daughter. I did something I had never done before. When the Pastor announced altar call, I got up, walked down the aisle, and knelt at the altar. There were times, in other churches, that I wanted to go to the altar for prayer, but I wouldn't go. This time, I was moved to go. I don't think I could have stopped myself if I had wanted to. I prayed like I had never prayed before. I still had a bit of that "Orphan mentality" about being cautious about who saw me cry, but that day, I cried like a baby. I fell on the floor and sobbed so hard I had to be helped back to my seat. I started going to church every Sunday. I considered joining the church, but I wasn't sure I was ready.

I hadn't attended church regularly in probably twenty years. I didn't need to go to church. Though somewhere in my psyche, a part of me always believed in God, I wasn't always sure that God believed in me. A part of me believed that God had abandoned me a long time ago, so I had no use for church or for God. But the more I thought about it, the more I realized that God had been with me my entire life.

And I began to reflect on my life, and how easily I could have lost it in that accident. It wasn't luck that saved my life. It was God. I began to better understand that God has a purpose for me. And in every situation, there is a blessing. People have been sent to me my entire life, in the darkest moments, just as Sis. Walker and Jack Mitchell were, who have comforted me, held me, and guided me.

Easter Sunday, 1998 started out like any other Sunday. My daughter and I went to church together. By this time, I was singing with the choir. When we got to the part of the service when "the doors of the church are opened," I started to step forward, but said, "No, not today." I sat there with my eyes closed and rocked from side to side as the musician played softly on the piano. I could feel the tears trickling down my face, and I heard a voice whisper in my ear, "Come to me." I walked in front of the altar, rededicated my life to God, and joined the church. First A.M.E. has been my church home ever since.

I am happier here than I ever was in Ohio. I miss my son,

my family, and my dear friends, but life here is good. It took a little longer than I expected, but I have a good job that I really enjoy. I've made new friends and am the surrogate grandmother to four young girls from my church. And of all the things I do, I think I like working with and being with the young people at my church more than anything.

And much like I did during my days in the Home, I still value my relationships more than I value anything else. If I lose my house, so what? If I lose my car, so what? If I lose my job, so what? Those can all be replaced. But if I lose someone I love, that loss will leave a hole in my heart that can never be filled again.

I have tried to write this book on three other occasions, the first time being 26 years ago. But it just wasn't right. It wasn't me. Then I realized that I didn't know who "me" was. I had buried my self so deep within myself that I wasn't sure if I would, or ever could come out of my shell.

Each of the next two versions was a little closer to what I wanted, but still not quite right. Then in August 1999, my church held a three-day revival. On the second night, I had a life-changing experience. There were issues that I thought had been resolved. They hadn't. I had merely tucked them away in a box labeled "Get Over It." But on that night, I stood face to face with my ghosts and demons. I felt as if I were in a battle for my soul. And I cried out, "Lord Jesus, help me."

And I felt the presence of the Holy Spirit in our little church. I felt the hands of God touching me and making me whole. I could feel the power of His blood, flowing through my veins healing my wounded spirit. I was literally knocked off my feet and was so in awe that I couldn't move. I just lay on the floor and cried.

For the next two weeks, I replayed that night over and over and over again. Being a bit of a skeptic, I tried to analyze and rationalize what had happened. But there were no tricks. There was no smoke and mirrors. This was something I had never experienced before. This was something real. I asked God for healing and I got it.

Then I began to write. It wasn't as if I made a conscious decision to do so. The words began to flow so effortlessly, one after the other. It was as if my hand was being guided by a will other than my own.

And I remembered something I learned from Jerrie, who entered my life in 1982 and has been my mother/sister/ friend ever since. She said, "Things don't always happen to us. Sometimes they happen for us." It took a while, but I finally understood what she meant. And through that realization, I have allowed the wounds to heal. Though the scars remain, the pain is subsiding.

# Chapter 20

❦

Had I not been in the Home, I don't know what my life may have been. I accept it for what it was and for what it is. From that insanity, I learned a lot about the kind of person I didn't want to be. I have spent most of my life trying not to be that. I just wasn't always sure who, or what I wanted to be.

I am now able to appreciate the advantages of having been in the Home. We attended one of the best schools in the state. We were never hungry. We always had clean clothes. We had warm beds and were never without water or electricity. Unlike a lot of children today, we weren't concerned about being bounced from home to home. And we forged relationship bonds that neither time nor distance can break.

And I've stopped blaming myself for situations over which I had no control. I have forgiven myself for the wrongs I've committed; and in so doing, I have freed myself to forgive those whom I believed have wronged me.

And maybe that's why I kept going back to the Home for the annual reunions. I think I was looking for closure, an apology or at least an explanation. And I didn't want that from Miss Allen, who made me feel like a dirty, devil child. I didn't want it from Belinda Logan or Miss Miller, who tried to beat me into submission. I didn't even want an apology from Miss Reutger for what she did to Buster. I wanted an apology from Mr. Williams. He was one of the few adults who really mattered to me. Because of that, he was one of the few who could, and ultimately did, really hurt me. On a conscious level, I knew an apology would never come, but subconsciously, I think I hoped it would.

I saw him at the 2001 Reunion. At nearly 80 years old, he seemed so small, almost frail. And I heard his apology. He didn't say, "Nancy, I'm sorry." He couldn't do that. And he didn't have to. We acknowledged each other from a distance and started walking toward each other. When I was close to him, he extended his hand. We spoke briefly. I never did shake his hand. Instead, we embraced. As we did, neither of us said a word. And in those few seconds of silence, I heard his apology and I believe he heard my acceptance and my forgiveness. We wished each other well and went our separate ways. I was finally able to close the book on that chapter of my life.

And Dee was there. The 2000 Reunion was her first in about twenty-five years. She was so excited when she went home that she got online and began to organize a big showing of our class for the 2001 Reunion. We had a decent turnout, thanks to her. Crystal was there too. I hadn't seen her in about thirty years. And Emma was there. And as we always do, we hugged and cried when we saw each other.

Dee, Emma, and I toured the campus together. The grass was badly in need of mowing. The trees and bushes were overgrown and almost obscured the locked doors to the cottages. Taft B was the first cottage we were able to enter. It was depressing. Though structurally sound, the cottage was a mess.

A dead bird was on the landing at the top of the steps, surrounded by paint chips that had fallen from the ceiling and the walls. The room I once shared with Betty and Dean had been converted to a kitchenette/dining room and was, surprisingly, in good shape. Mrs. Vincent's quarters were damp and musty. The carpet was filthy. The paint on the walls was bubbled and peeling. The walls were covered with scuff marks and cobwebs graced every corner. I couldn't go any further than the office. What would Mrs. Vincent think, what would she say if she could see the condition of her cottage?

We went upstairs. The door to the room Emma and I shared was unlocked, one of only two doors that were. The room was empty and so small. The mirror above the built-in dresser was gone. Two of the dresser drawers were warped and wouldn't close. It was hard to believe that the two of us were able to fit all of our earthly possessions into that tiny closet and one four-drawer dresser.

As I stood in the middle of the room, I could hear the clicking of the canes we won at the Greene County Fair as we lay in bed and had sword fights at night. I could hear the voices of teenaged girls whispering and giggling about anything, everything, and nothing during our mandatory rest periods on Saturday and Sunday afternoons. I could hear the faint tiptoe-ing of footsteps in the hall as we exchanged copies of Reader's Digest and contraband True Confession Magazines. I found myself smiling. And while Emma told Dee about the time that she accidentally mooned me, I was laughing aloud.

I said a silent goodbye to my room and walked down the hall. The green door to the A side was open. There was an overturned chair, several boxes, and other junk in the hall. I stepped over the threshold, stood there for about five seconds, turned around, and walked back down the hall. Although I had spent about a year in Taft A, I had no desire to see the cottage. I crossed over to the A side simply because there was no one there to tell me that I couldn't!

We left the cottage shaking our heads. Dee and I were quiet and Emma just kept saying, "What a shame. What a shame."

We toured the rest of the girls' side, then walked to the farm. We couldn't get to the barn. Some tree trimmers were busy at work and their truck blocked the road. We headed for Peter Pan.

What a heart-wrenching sight that was. While the State tried to decide what to do with the property after the Home closed in 1995, the FBI used Peter Pan for training exercises. They set off explosives that left gaping holes in the buildings. The hole in Pan 3 was large enough that I could have stepped through the brick wall, from the outside, and stood in the living room. The dining room looked like a scene from a World War II movie. The devastation was deplorable and absolutely unbelievable.

Pan 6 was locked. We were disappointed, but that may have been a good thing. I don't think I could have taken it if Pan 6 looked anything like Pan 3. There was a softball-sized hole in the roof. The windows were boarded, but the facade was still intact.

As we headed back toward the main campus, we said very little. Dee, who had never lived in Peter Pan, understood our pain and shared our silence.

When we got back on campus, we sat on benches on the parade field and talked for hours. Several Orphans from our class and their spouses joined us. We posed on the steps of the auditorium for class photos. We inducted the spouses as Honorary Orphans and they posed with us. We laughed as we looked at old pictures and we shared information about other Orphans who didn't make Reunion.

The conversation took a serious turn when we started talking about relationships. RW beautifully summarized what we all felt. Many years ago, he took a sociology class. On the first day, the professor asked the students to introduce themselves and tell a little about their families. One student said he had five brothers and sisters. Someone else said she had three brothers and sisters. When it was RW's turn, he said, "I have over 600 brothers and sisters." Of course, the whole class wondered what that meant. And he obliged by telling them about the Home.

We've all grown and changed a lot over the years. Most of my classmates have grown children and some of us are enjoying our grandchildren. But we cling to the friendships we formed during our years in the Home. And no matter how long we live, those friendships will remain as strong and as constant as they were when we were children.

◇

I still am not the person I hope to be. But praise God, I am not the person I had to become in order to survive. I have gone back in time, dug deep into my center, and I have found the person I am suppose to be, the person God intended for me to be. And as life goes on, I continue to change and to grow, for this is an ever-changing, on-going journey that will continue for as long as I have breath.

So, in the meantime, I continue to stumble, but I continue to get up. I continue fall short, but I continue to succeed. I continue to question, but I continue to believe. I continue the journey, the journey to me.

It has been an interesting ride. And as difficult as it has been sometimes, the lessons I've learned are invaluable. And when I look at where I am and what I've accomplished, I think about some adults from my childhood and wonder what they would think. Mrs. Neville might be a little disappointed that I never became a nurse. I think Mrs. Black would be pleased to know that I still write. Mr. Rooney would be thrilled to know that I have had some success as a professional actress and have had three of my plays produced. And I believe Mr. Williams was genuinely happy to know that I am all right.

Sis. Walker would be glad to know that the frightened little girl with the tear-stained face is a woman who is no longer afraid and has found peace. And she would delight in the fact that I have reconnected with a church and work with the children. How I wish I could tell her how much the memory of her love and nurturing sustained me throughout the years.

And I think my mother would be proud of the woman I have become. After all these years, I still miss her and wish I could have known her.

And though I don't really need one, I wish I had a blue popsicle right now—just for old times' sake.

# Dedication

༃

Dedicated with love to Buster

Walter Steve Gibson
February 1952 – October 1979

I told you that I would remember,
and I promised you that I would tell.

I kept that promise.

# A History in Brief

⅗

1869 Grand Army of the Republic founds the Ohio Soldiers' & Sailors' Orphans' (OS&SO) Home.

1874 Superintendent resigns after "morals charge" investigation.

1875 Fire destroys Grant Building (Main Building).

1879 Renovated Grant Building opens.

1881 Staff member's involvement in scandal prompts investigation.

120 former students attend First Annual Reunion.

1893 Student enrollment hits an all-time high at 914.

1907 Attempts to place the Home under State supervision and management fail.

1911 Home exempted from law requiring all State institutions to be under the control of a central board.

1920 Home's military instructor enforces commands by "brute strength," including "a swift kick in the seat of the pants".

Only 9% of 617 children are orphans.

1930 Children stop military-style marching to classes, and begin wearing civilian clothes.

1935 Governor's Committee concludes educational level at the Home is substandard.

1955 Association of Ex-Pupils (AXP) host 75th Annual Reunion, with 750 former students attending.
Track team wins State title.

1956 Integration of cottages begins when Nancy Gibson moves to Peter Pan.

1959 State legislators note outdated childcare practices. Costs continue to rise while enrollment falls.

1960 Integration of cottages on the main campus begins.

1963 The Pride of Ohio, a history of the OS&SO Home, is completed.
The Little Hoover Commission, 88 businessmen, concludes study and recommends cost-savings measures. Also recommends placing the Home under the State's Youth Services Division and abolishing the Home's Board of Trustees. Recommendations ignored.

1967 Blacks, mostly from Central State and Wilberforce Universities, demand principal's resignation, saying that he mistreated a black female. Although he admitted striking and kicking Nancy Gibson during a disciplinary session, a jury finds him innocent of assault.

1973 Ohio State University study recommends that the Home change its mission to meet changing needs of children.

1977 Less than 5% of 197 children are orphans.

1978 Home's name changes to Ohio Veterans' Children's Home. Being a child of a veteran is no longer mandatory.

1981 The Home's Farm ceases operations.

1985 Enrollment drops to 135.

1987 State Attorney General's Office issues statement: "The Home doesn't have to follow policies of other juvenile residential institutions." (Home's Board of Trustees member is a top aide to the Attorney General).

1988    EEOC study concludes that the Home has too few women and minorities in professional positions.

Assistant Dean resigns just before being indicted on three counts of sexual battery. Pleads guilty to one count; receives probation.

1989    Janitor pleads guilty to contributing to the delinquency of minors. Receives probation.

Special grand jury convened in investigation of 250 allegations reported a small group of employees. Nine indictments issued next day.

1990    Superintendent charged with one count of obstructing justice and four counts of failure to report child abuse.

Nine former and current employees indicted on charges including child abuse, child endangering, sexual abuse, rape, and theft.

1991    Rape charge against former teacher dropped in exchange for guilty plea to two counts of sexual battery. Receives probation and ordered to get counseling.

1992    Home changes age requirements. Will not accept any child under the age of 13. Enrollment limited to 100 children.

Board of Trustees abolished. Home now operates under the State Board of Control.

First female Superintendent appointed.

1993    Superintendent fired because of poor financial management.

1995    The Ohio Veterans' Children's Home/OS&SO Home closes.

1997    Ownership shifts from the State of Ohio to Greene County.

County leases 9.2 acres to the AXP until 2020. AXP maintains the Museum, the Band Shell, the Collier Chapel and cemetery.

1998 Dayton Christian Schools' bid on 253 acres approved. Legacy Ministries International forms as an umbrella organization to own and operate the Home. Plans for the facility include: Xenia Christian School; The International School Project; WFCJ satellite broadcast studio; International Institute for Christian Education; Summer Camps; Residential Housing; Legacy Village, a senior citizens' complex; a Home for Unwed Mothers; Athletes in Action; and Staff Housing.

1999 Xenia Christian School opens on Home grounds.

*Sources*: *The Pride of Ohio; Dayton Daily News, Journal Herald,* and *Xenia Gazette* historical clippings; OSSO/OVCH records